THE JEAN MOSS BOOK OF
WORLD KNITS

THE JEAN MOSS BOOK OF
WORLD KNITS

The Taunton Press

Cover photo: **JACK DEUTSCH**

Taunton
BOOKS & VIDEOS
for fellow enthusiasts

Printed in the United States of America
10 9 8 7 6 5 4 3 2 1

A THREADS Book
THREADS® is a trademark of The Taunton Press, Inc.,
registered in the U.S. Patent and Trademark Office.

The Taunton Press, Inc., 63 South Main Street, P.O. Box 5506,
Newtown, CT 06470-5506
e-mail: tp@taunton.com

Library of Congress Cataloging-in-Publication Data

Moss, Jean.
    The Jean Moss book of world knits / Jean Moss.
       p.   cm.
    "A Threads book"—T.p. verso.
    ISBN 1-56158-198-4
    1. Knitting—Patterns. 2. Knit goods. I. Title.
TT825.M6828 1997
746.43'2041—dc21   97-24049
                                 CIP

FOR PHILIP, FOR ALL
THOSE HOURS OF WOOL
WINDING!
AND SO MUCH MORE...

ACKNOWLEDGMENTS

I'd like to thank the many people who have helped me with this book. There are too many to name all, but there are a few I must mention.

First, my warmest thanks to all the knitters: Denise Andrews, Ann Banks, Mrs. Brigham, Peggy Burglin, Jean Clare, Mary Coe, Betty Falconer, Mrs. Fowler, Glennis Garnett, Anne Hart, Carol Henderson, Jenny Poole, Mrs. Veale, Yvonne Rawlinson, and Jean Wilson. Your beautiful work is much appreciated.

Thanks to Rowan for its splendid natural yarn, and to Elizabeth, Karen, and Nicola for sending it out so efficiently.

Thanks to Galer Brittan-Barnes for her Brittany hardwood knitting needles—I knitted all the swatches with them and found the needles a joy to work with.

David Palmer-Jones' wonderful Tibetan buttons continue to be a treasure, finishing off the sweaters perfectly.

Warm thanks to Catherine Cobb, hat designer, for making the felted hats. A visit to her wonderful shop, Ipseity, is a must for any hat freak visiting York.

A big thank you to Suzette Bergeron for taking the time, over supper at her mum Valerie's home, to teach me how to make socks. Thanks also to Priscilla A. Gibson-Roberts for her excellent book *Ethnic Socks and Stockings* and to Nancy Bush for *Folk Socks*. These are two books on sock construction that I have referred to at length.

Many thanks to Sheila Paine, who offered to lend textiles from her collection for the book. I owe a huge debt to her superb book *Embroidered Textiles*, which was a great source and compulsive reading on textiles and symbolism.

Warmest thanks to John Gillow, who generously lent some of his best African textiles from his fabulous collection. Thanks also to Kate Lofthouse for lending me her glorious Dajan dress. My thanks also to The Castle Museum, York; The National Museum of Ireland, Dublin; and Gordon Reece Gallery, Knaresborough, for their cooperation on this project.

Thank you to Ken and June Bridewater at Westminster Fibers for their support and help and for all the hard work they do promoting designers and needlecrafts with their workshop tours.

Grateful thanks to Susan Lazear of the Cochenille Design Studio for her wonderful computer program, Stitch Painter, and to Gillian Lamb for so patiently taking the time to sort out the initial teething problems.

Lastly, I must thank all the retailers who believe in knitting and have the vision to ride out the hard times and stick with it. People need only two knitting needles, inspiring yarn, and a little instruction to create something beautiful. Yarn stores, like Mary McGurn's Colourful Stitches in Lenox, which provides a stylish, stimulating, and supportive environment, do an excellent job of promoting the art of knitting. From what I saw on a recent tour of the United States, there are many such dedicated stores, and I'm sure knitting will only go on and up!

Thanks again to all of you.

CONTENTS

INTRODUCTION

For as long as I can remember, I have had a passion for textiles. From intricate English samplers to exotic Banjara altar cloths, from labyrinthine Shoowa raffia embroideries to beautiful Palestinian wedding dresses, every culture has its tradition of decorative textile art, each imbued with its own folk-lore, history, and meaning. These ethnic patterns share a worldwide symbolic language and offer rich pickings for the designer.

Geometric shapes, such as the triangle, diamond, zigzag, and eight-pointed star, are sources of magical protection and have variously denoted fertility, health, prosperity, and happiness through the generations and across cultures. These shapes form the building blocks of primi-tive patterns from as far back as the Paleolithic period to modern times. The hand and fish symbols are widespread as protection against the evil eye. The crescent, spiral, and circle shapes are potent symbols of the cosmic force of the sun and moon and of the motion and rein-vention of life.

Color has always been crucial. There are three colors that are consistently used to denote the continuity of the human life cycle: red, the color that predominates in many old textiles, is a symbol for life, fire, the sun, and power and is used for protection; white denotes birth, purity, and the celestial; and black represents decay and death.

Textiles are one of humankind's earliest forms of artistic expression. They are a marvelous way of learning about civiliza-tions and cultures way back into prehistory. There is such a wealth of history in a piece of cloth. Many designs have been made for centuries in the same way, decorated with the same symbols that have been handed down from generation to generation. Although many of the ancient meanings have been lost, it is fortunate that the patterns have prevailed.

A textile says so much about the life of the person who made it, and it can encap-sulate a culture. I love holding a piece of history in my hand and pondering its ori-gin. I'm fascinated that the same symbols are used by peoples who have always been separated by thousands of miles, such as the labyrinths of the Shoowa people of Congo and the knots of the Celts of Ireland. It is as if there is a common consciousness expressed in clothes and furnishings. How exciting it is to be able to appreciate these universal patterns in a piece of cloth that not only displays a mastery of its medium but also carries within it the evolution and development of its creators.

It is hugely satisfying to have the oppor-tunity to share in and contribute to this massive pool of human creativity. It gives me enormous pleasure to work with these ancient shapes and patterns and to produce contemporary pieces inspired by them. In this book, I shall look at some glorious works of decorative embroidery, needlepoint, and weaving, and I shall explain how these pieces can be used as springboards to new designs. I feel it is important to retain the essence of a pattern rather than to slavishly copy it. I try to pinpoint the fundamental attraction the textile has for me and the key to the effortless balance, beauty, and sense of harmony that many old textiles radiate. I use this key to open a door to a new and often quite different design.

There are endless unique and wonderful sweaters waiting to be designed using the gold mine of traditional textiles. Folk art is essentially people's art, and I do believe that within every person there is an innate ability to craft beautiful artifacts. I'm pleased to share these new patterns with you, for although each piece is an expression of my creativity, I feel it also has its foundation in a greater whole. In this book, I hope that you will find my contributions to world textiles inspiring, just as I did with the textiles that I have used as sources for the projects.

There are projects to suit all levels of knitting expertise, time, and pocket. A beautiful pillow, hat, or pair of socks, lovingly crafted in the otherwise wasted hours traveling to work, makes a great gift. One of the wonderful things about knitting is that it is very portable. It can provide an oasis into which you can retreat in a stressful situation—it is a familiar friend. Knitting is, as I'm sure you all know, a splendid stress reliever! For knitters with a little more time, there are sweaters, jackets, and throws, too.

Just a word about buttons. The sweaters are finished with hand-carved buttons in wood, brass, bone, and horn made in Kathmandu. Beautiful buttons are so important to a sweater. They can make the difference between an attractive garment and a stunning one! I have chosen geometric shapes and the figurative symbols of the fish, hand, and sun both to complement the sweaters and to continue the theme of the collection.

I do hope you will enjoy knitting my patterns inspired by these traditional textiles of our world. Always remember that, if you wish, you can add something of your own to make the design unique, your contribution to world knits!

Happy knitting. I'm looking forward to seeing your projects.

ABBREVIATIONS

alt	alternate		m1	make one—pick up loop between sts and knit into back of it
approx	approximately			
beg	begin(ning)			
ch	chain stitch		mm	millimeter(s)
cm	centimeter(s)		oz.	ounce(s)
cn	cable needle		p	purl
cont	continu(e)(ing)		patt(s)	pattern(s)
c2b	cross 2 back—knit into back of second st on needle, then knit first st, slipping both sts off needle together		pb1	purl into back of next st
			pbf	increase by purling into back and front of purl st
			psso	pass slipped stitch over
			rem	remain(s)(ing)
c2p	cross 2 purl—purl into front of second st on needle, then purl first st, slipping both sts off needle together		rep	repeat(s)(ing)
			rev	revers(e)(ing)
			rev st st	reverse stockinette stitch
			RH	right hand
			rnd	round
cr2bp	slip next st onto cn, hold back, kb1, p1 from cn		RS	right side(s)
			sl	slip
cr2fk	slip next st onto cn, hold at front, p1, kb1 from cn		ssk	slip 1 st as if to knit, slip another st as if to knit, then knit these 2 sts together
dc	double crochet			
dec	decreas(e)(ing)		st(s)	stitch(es)
dia	diameter		st st	stockinette stitch
foll	follow(s)(ing)		tbl	through back of loop(s)
g	grams		tog	together
in.	inch(es)		tr	treble crochet
inc	increase(e)(ing)		WS	wrong side(s)
k	knit		yb	yarn back
k1b	insert needle through center of st below next st on needle and knit in the usual way, slipping the st above off the needle at the same time		yd.	yard(s)
			yf	yarn forward
			yo	yarn over
			*	repeat instructions after asterisk or between asterisks as many times as instructed
kb1	knit into back of next st			
kfb	increase by knitting into front and back of knit st		( )	repeat instructions inside parentheses as many times as instructed
LH	left hand			
m	meter(s)			

KNITTING NEEDLE SIZES

U.S.	Metric	Old U.K.
0	2mm	14
1	2.25mm	13
2	2.75	12
	3mm	11
3	3.25mm	10
4	3.5mm	
5	3.75mm	9
6	4mm	8
7	4.5mm	7
8	5mm	6
9	5.5mm	5
10	6mm	4
10.5	6.5mm	3
	7mm	2
	7.5mm	1
11	8mm	0

YARN INFORMATION

When possible, use the yarn recommended in the knitting pattern instructions. If you wish to use a substitute yarn, choose one of the same type and weight as the recommended yarn. Use the following descriptions of the various Rowan yarns as a guide. To calculate the amount of yarn needed, determine the number of meters or yards required rather than the number of grams or ounces. Your yarn shop will be able to assist you if you have difficulty in choosing a suitable substitute.

Rowan True 4-ply Botany
100% pure new wool, machine washable, approx 170m per 50g ball

Rowan Donegal Lambswool Tweed
100% pure new wool, approx 112m per 25g hank

Rowan Kid Silk
70% mohair, 30% silk, approx 64m per 25g ball

Rowan Lurex
75% viscose, 25% lurex, approx 57m per 25g hank

Rowan DK Marl
100% pure new wool, approx 130m per 50g hank

Rowan Lightweight Double Knitting
100% pure new wool, approx 67m per 25g hank

Rowan Designer Double Knitting
100% pure new wool, approx 115m per 50g balls

Rowan Magpie Aran
100% pure new wool, approx 140m per 100g hank

Rowan Magpie Tweed
100% pure wool, approx 170m per 100g hank

Rowan Cotton Glacé
100% cotton, approx 112m per 50g ball

Rowan Handknit DK Cotton
100% cotton, approx 82m per 50g ball

Rowan Denim Cotton DK
100% cotton, approx 93m per 50g ball

Rowan Chunky Cotton Chenille
100% cotton, approx 140m per 100g ball

Rowan Fine Cotton Chenille
85% cotton, 15% polyester, approx 160m per 50g ball

KIT INFORMATION

Most designs are available as kits either from your local Rowan retailer or by mail order from Jean Moss, 17 Clifton Dale, York YO3 6LJ.
Phone/fax: 01904 646282
e-mail: moss@dircon.co.uk
For the order form and prices, see p. 151.

COLORWORK NOTES

Charts are read from right to left on RS rows and from left to right on WS rows.

Fairisle knitting
When working two colors on a row, loosely strand or weave the color not in use on WS. Do not strand the yarn over more than 3 sts and take care that the overall tension does not change or pull in the work.

Intarsia knitting
When working a pattern, use a separate ball of yarn each time a new color occurs and twist this yarn around the previous color to avoid holes. Use short lengths of yarn (no longer than 18 in. unless you are working large color blocks) so that the yarn does not become tangled.

Intarsia knitting in the round
Work as above on RS rounds, but on WS rounds turn the work at the end of each color block. Purl back to the beginning of the block (as if knitting back and forth), twisting the yarns as above at the end of each block and slipping these stitches on the RS rounds.

STITCH INSTRUCTIONS

Straight wrap cast on

Hold two needles side by side in your left hand. Beginning at left with a short tail in front, take the yarn behind then over the top needle, wrapping counterclockwise around the two needles and ending with the yarn going under the bottom needle and coming out to the front (see the top illustration at left below). With the yarn held in place around the bottom needle, knit the top stitches (see the center illustration at left below). At the end of this row, the tail yarn should be securely wrapped around the working yarn or the end stitch will be easily lost. Rotate the needles and knit the stitches in the top position (see the bottom illustration at left below).

Backward loop cast on

Using the thumb method and one needle, loop each stitch onto the needle without knitting it, rotating the thumb under the yarn and toward you in a clockwise motion before slipping the stitch onto the needle.

Two-color cast on

With the tail at the back, bring the first color yarn between two needles, then down to the back. Bring the yarn up and over both needles to the back again, then up and over and between the needles to the back (see the top illustration at right below). To change color, lay the second color yarn over the first. Take the second color up and between the needles and wrap as before (see the center illustration at right below). Drop the second color, then lay the first color over the second. Repeat the wrap (see the bottom illustration at right below). When all stitches have been wrapped on the needles, take the second color around the last yarn used, thus securing the last loop. Maintaining the color sequence, knit across the top stitches. Rotate the needles clockwise and knit, twisting the yarns at the edge to secure as before. Continue in this manner, working three rounds and maintaining the color pattern.

STRAIGHT WRAP CAST ON

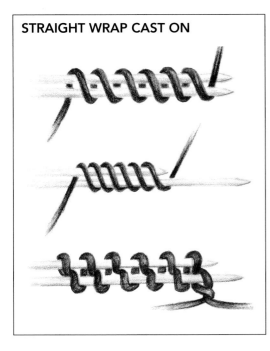

TWO-COLOR CAST ON

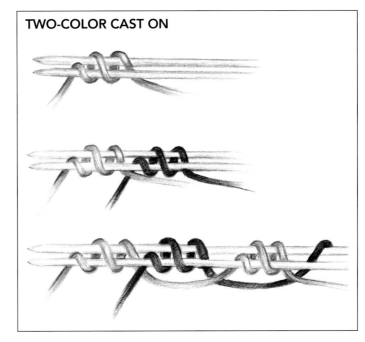

Continental cast on

Make a slip knot and place it on the RH needle, leaving a long tail (leave enough length for the number of stitches you will need to cast on for your sock). Place your left thumb and index finger between the two threads. Secure the long ends with your other three fingers. Twist your wrist so your palm faces upward, and spread your thumb and index finger to make a V of the yarn around them (see the top left illustration).

Insert the needle into the yarn around your thumb from front to back. Place the needle over the yarn around your index finger (see the top right illustration). Bring the needle down through the loop around your thumb (see the bottom left illustration). Drop the loop off your thumb and, placing your thumb back in the V configuration, tighten the resulting stitch on the needle (see the bottom right illustration). Repeat this process until all the stitches are cast on.

CONTINENTAL CAST ON

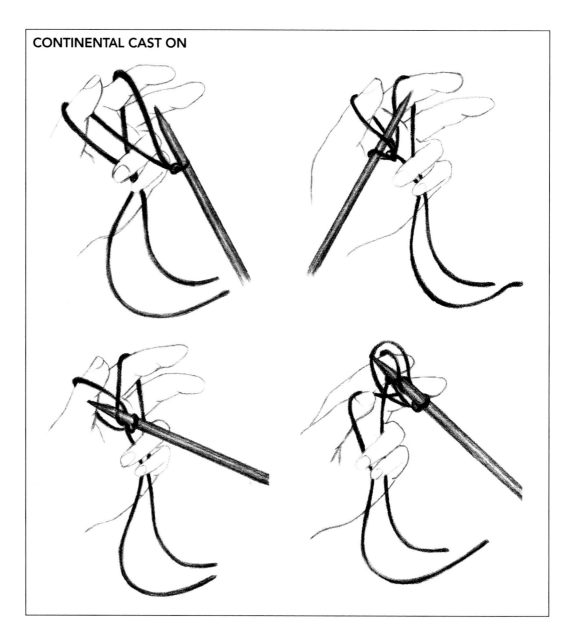

Kitchener stitch

Hold the two needles parallel and close together with the yarn coming from the RH end of the top needle. Break the yarn, leaving a 10-in. end. Thread the yarn onto a tapestry needle.

*Pull the yarn through the first stitch on the bottom needle as if to knit and slip the stitch off the needle. Pull the yarn through the second stitch of the bottom needle as if to purl and leave the stitch on the needle. Pull the yarn through the first stitch of the top needle as if to purl and slip the stitch off the needle. Pull the yarn through the second stitch of the top needle as if to knit and leave the stitch on the needle (see the illustration at right). Repeat from * until all stitches are used up. Weave in the end and snip it off.

KITCHENER STITCH

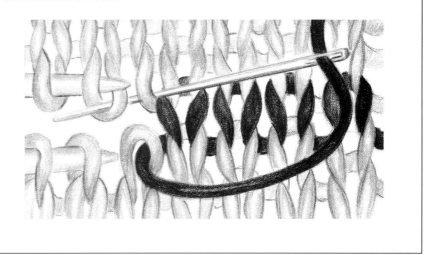

Double crochet (U.S. single crochet)

Holding the crochet hook in your right hand and the yarn in your left, start with one loop on the hook. Insert the hook through the top of the stitch to the left of the hook, yarn over, and draw the loop through. You now have two loops on the crochet hook. Yarn over and draw through both loops on the hook. Insert hook in next stitch and repeat.

DOUBLE CROCHET

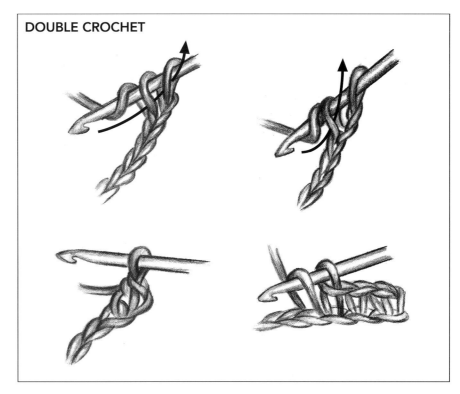

SHOOWA

SWEATER

WAISTCOAT

THROW

HAT

The Shoowa people from the kingdom of Kuba, in what is now Congo, have been designing and making beautiful textiles such as the one shown above for hundreds of years. The intricate, cut-pile raffia embroideries in bold, earthy colors have a variety of uses. Originally used as seat covers, the embroideries are also used as currency, dowries, status symbols, and even shrouds. What particularly excites me about them is not only their infinite labyrinths—the layering of geometric shapes to create patterns within pattern—but also the striking similarity of their knots and mazes to ancient Celtic designs.

In the Shoowa sweater, throw, and hat, I have taken the interlocking diamond theme and worked it into an aran cable as the backdrop for the geometric patterns that typify Shoowa embroideries. This offers a perfect context for my love of mixing texture and color. Many of these textiles incorporate a striped zigzag in their designs, and I have reflected this at the welts. For one of the sweater's colorways, I have deliberately chosen the symbolic

colors of red, white, and black. Not only does this create a striking visual impact, but it also associates the sweater with the universal themes of the human condition—protection, life, and death. There are infinite possibilities for substituting another color for the red while keeping the black and white. The colorways are all inter-changeable. For those who prefer to knit in one color only, these designs will still look fabulous if you choose a sculptured stitch to pick out the patterns within the cables.

In the Shoowa waistcoat, the diamond theme is used again, combined with zigzags to create an intricate, flat-knit labyrinth of intarsia design. Although I would not recommend this piece to an inexperienced knitter, it is a very satisfying sweater to complete. As it is a smallish project, it would be an interesting challenge for experienced knitters who want to try intarsia knitting. I hope you will experi-ment and substitute stitches and colorways of your own to create a truly unique work inspired by the wonderful embroideries of the Shoowa.

SWEATER

Shoowa sweater in cotton

NEEDLES

Cotton version:
• 3.25mm (USA 3)
• 4mm (USA 6)
• Set of four 3mm (USA 2)
• Cable needle

Wool version:
• 3.75mm (USA 5)
• 4.5mm (USA 7)
• Set of four 3.25mm (USA 3)
• Cable needle

TENSION

24 sts and 30 rows = 4 in. or 10cm over patt

SIZES

Two sizes to fit 34-in. to 40-in. (40-in. to 46-in.) bust
See diagram on p. 15 for finished knitted measurements.

YARN

Rowan DK Cotton (cotton version); Rowan Designer DK (wool version)

	Key		Color	Quantity	
Cotton version	☐	A	Red 215	18 (20) balls	x 50g
	Ⓞ	B	Black 252	4 (5) balls	x 50g
	Ⓥ	C	Ecru 251	2 (2) balls	x 50g
	Ⓩ	D	Black 252		
	⊡	E	Ecru 251		
	Ⓢ	F	Ecru 251		
	◪	G	Black 252		
	☒	H	Ecru 251		
	⊞	I	Black 252		
Wool version	☐	A	Damson 659	13 (15) balls	x 50g
	Ⓞ	B	Rust 663	3 (4) balls	x 50g
	Ⓥ	C	Burgundy 637	1 ball	x 50g
	Ⓩ	D	Olive 639	1 ball	x 50g
	⊡	E	Teal Green 661	1 ball	x 50g
	Ⓢ	F	Taupe 698	1 ball	x 50g
	◪	G	Celadon 685	1 ball	x 50g
	☒	H	Old Gold 690	1 ball	x 50g
	⊞	I	Cinnamon 691	1 ball	x 50g

Previous page: Shoowa throw in colorway 2 and sweater in wool

AFGHAN STITCH

Row 1 (RS) Using col A, k1, ssk, *k13, (sl2-k1-p2sso), rep from * to last 16 sts, k13, k2tog, k1.

Row 2 Using col A, k1, *p1, k6, (k1, yo, k1) in next st, k6, rep from * to last 2 sts, p1, k1.

Rows 3 and 4 Using col B, rep rows 1 and 2.

BACK

Using col B and 3.25mm needles for the cotton version or 3.75mm for the wool, cast on 147 (163 for larger size) sts and work 1 row. Using afghan stitch, work 20 rows, rep the 4 rows 5 times.

ROW 21 Using col A, k1, ssk, *k14, ssk, rep from * to last 16 sts, k16 (138 sts). For larger size, omit first ssk (154 sts).

FOR COTTON VERSION: Change to 4mm needles. Foll chart 1 on the facing page, work the 146 rows, starting row 1 on a purl row and reading from left to right.

FOR WOOL VERSION: Change to 4.5mm needles. Foll chart 1, work the 188 rows, starting on row 71 on a purl row and reading from left to right. Work to row 112, then work the 146 rows from row 1.

FOR BOTH VERSIONS: For larger size, work an extra 8 sts in set patt at each side.
Foll chart 1, shape neckline on row 143, leaving center 34 sts on a st holder.

FRONT

Work as for back, but foll chart 1 on the facing page for neckline shaping on row 128, leaving center 20 sts on a st holder.

146 140 130 120 110 100 90 80 70 60 50 40 30 20 10

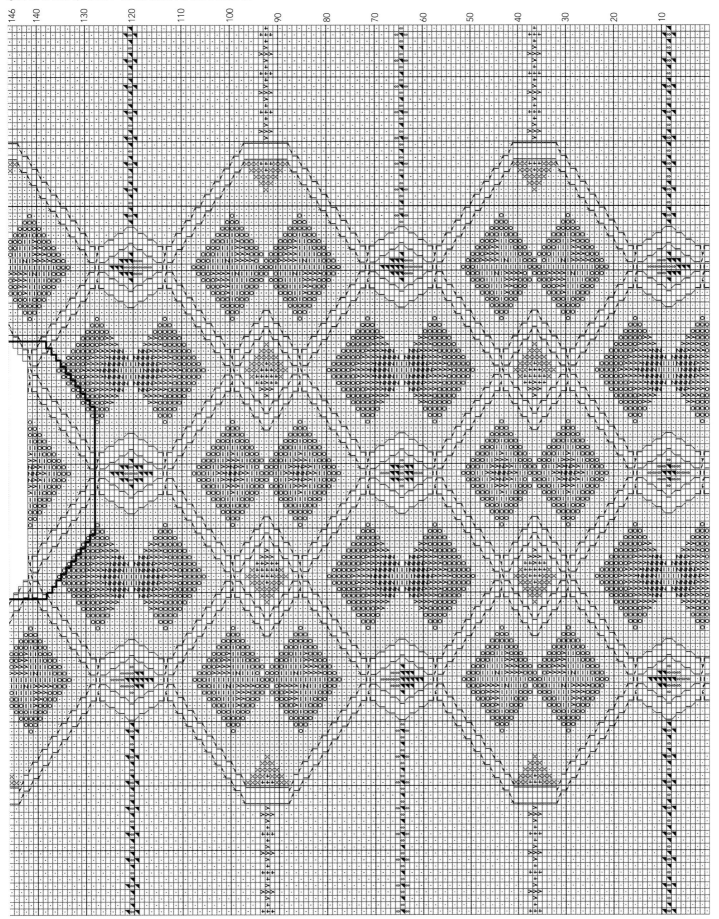

SWEATER CHART 2: SLEEVE

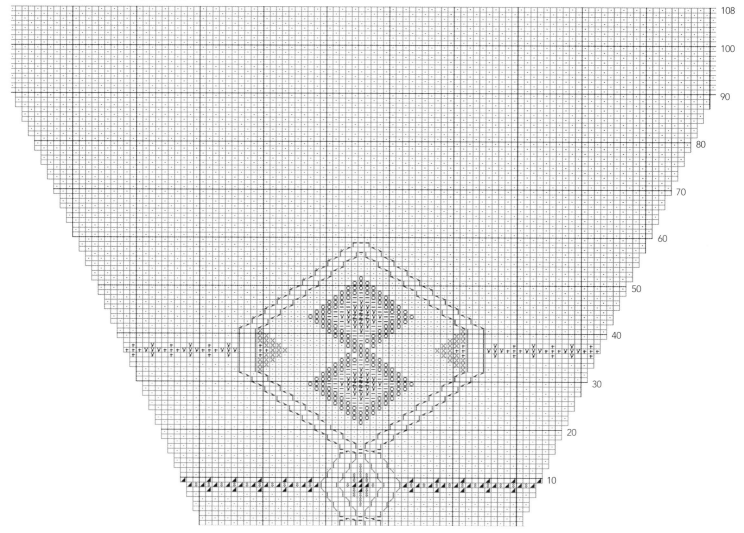

SWEATER STITCH KEY

⊡   rev st st—purl on RS and knit on WS

3 over 3 cross (over 7 sts)—sl 4 sts to cn and hold at front, k3, sl the center st from cn back to LH needle and purl it, then k3 from cn

3 over 3 cross (over 7 sts)—sl 4 sts to cn and hold at back, k3, sl the center st from cn back to LH needle and purl it, then k3 from cn

3 over 1 cross (over 4 sts)—sl 3 sts to cn and hold at front, p1, then k3 from cn

3 over 1 cross (over 4 sts)—sl 1 st to cn and hold at back, k3, then p1 from cn

3 over 2 cross (over 5 sts)—sl 3 sts to cn and hold at front, p2, then k3 from cn

3 over 2 cross (over 5 sts)—sl 2 sts to cn and hold at back, k3, then p2 from cn

Note: All the above cable crossings occur on knit rows as chart starts on purl row (reading from left to right)

SLEEVES

Using col B and 3.25mm needles for the cotton version or 3.75mm for the wool, cast on 51 sts and work 1 row. Using afghan stitch, work 20 rows.

ROW 21 Knit.
Change to 4mm needles for the cotton version or 4.5mm for the wool. Foll chart 2 on the facing page, work the 108 rows, starting row 1 on a purl row and inc 1 st at both ends of every third row until there are 111 sts. Cont to end of chart or until work measures 18 in. Cast off.

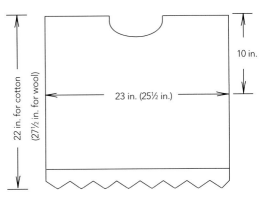

NECKBAND

With RS facing and using a small, neat back-stitch on edge of work, join shoulder seams. Using col A and four double-pointed 3mm needles for the cotton version or 3.25mm for the wool, start at left front shoulder seam with RS facing. Pick up and knit 18 sts down front neck edge; 20 sts from spare needle at center front; 18 sts up other side neck edge to shoulder; 3 sts down back neck edge; 34 sts from spare needle at center back; and 3 sts up back neck edge (96 sts).
Working in the round (all rows knit rows), proceed as follows:

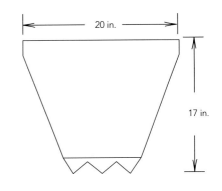

RND 1 *K1, p1, k1, p1, k4, rep from * around.

RND 2 *K1, p1, k1, p1, k1, p3, rep from * around.
Rep these 2 rnds until neckband measures 2½ in., ending on rnd 2.
Change to col B and work a further 2 rnds as above. Cast off loosely.

FINISHING

Use a small, neat backstitch on edge of work for all seams. Mark 10 in. down from shoulder on back and front side edges and insert sleeves between these marks. Join side and sleeve seams in one line from top of afghan stitch to top of afghan stitch. Join afghan stitch using an invisible slipstitch so that it lies flat.

Shoowa waistcoat in colorway 2

WAISTCOAT

NEEDLES
• 2.75mm (USA 2)
• 3.25mm (USA 3)
• 2.75mm (USA 2) circular

BUTTONS
Five 14mm

TENSION
28 sts and 40 rows = 4 in. or 10cm over patt

SIZE
One size to fit 32-in. to 40-in. bust
See diagram on p. 19 for finished knitted measurements.

AFGHAN STITCH
Row 1 (RS) Using col C, k1, ssk, *k13, (sl2-k1-p2sso), rep from * to last 16 sts, k13, k2tog, k1.
Row 2 Using col C, k1, *p1, k6, (k1, yo, k1) in next st, k6, rep from * to last 2 sts, p1, k1.
Rows 3 and 4 Using col B, rep rows 1 and 2.

BACK
Using 3.25mm needles and col B, cast on 143 sts and knit 1 row. Using afghan stitch, work 16 rows, rep the 4 rows 4 times.
Foll chart 1 on p. 18, rep the 44 sts across row, centering the chart thus:

ROW 1 (RS) Working from right to left, work the last 5 sts, work the 44 sts 3 times, work the first 6 sts (143 sts).

ROW 2 Working from left to right, work the last 6 sts, work the 44 sts 3 times, work the first 5 sts (143 sts).
Rep the 40 rows of the chart throughout the back, inc 1 st at both ends of every sixth row until there are 169 sts, keeping patt correct. When patt will read: Work the last 18 sts, work the 44 sts 3 times, work the first 19 sts (169 sts). Cont until work measures 12 in. from cast-on edge and ends with a WS row.

YARN
Rowan Donegal Lambswool Tweed (cols A, B, D, E, F, G); Rowan 4-ply Botany (col C); Rowan Kid Silk (col H)

Key		Colorway 1	Colorway 2	Quantity	
☐	A	Bramble 484	Dolphin 478	3 hanks	x 25g
◻	B	Cinnamon 479	Sapphire 486	3 hanks	x 25g
⊙	C	Redwood 549	Leaf 481	1 ball	x 50g
⊞	D	Sapphire 486	Tarragon 477	3 hanks	x 25g
⊡	E	Juniper 482	Marram 472	2 hanks	x 25g
△	F	Roseberry 480	Eau-de-nil 458	2 hanks	x 25g
⊠	G	Pickle 483	Juniper 482	3 hanks	x 25g
⊠	H	Old Gold 989	Old Gold 989	1 ball	x 25g

SHAPE ARMHOLE Cast off 7 sts at beg of next 2 rows. Then dec 1 st at both ends of next and every row until there are 109 sts, keeping patt correct. Cont in patt as set until work measures 22½ in. from cast-on edge and ends with a WS row.

SHAPE NECKLINE Cast off 11 sts at beg of next row, work 26 sts, and leave rem 72 sts on a st holder. Working one side only, dec 1 st at beg of next row and work to end. Cast off 11 sts at beg of next row and work to last 2 sts, k2tog. Dec 1 st at beg of next row and work to end. Cast off rem 12 sts. Leave the center 35 sts on a st holder. Rejoin yarn to neck edge and work to end of row. Cast off 11 sts at beg of next row and work to last 2 sts, k2tog. Dec 1 st at beg of next row and work to end. Cast off 11 sts at beg of next row and work to last 2 sts, k2tog. Work 1 row. Cast off rem 12 sts.

RIGHT FRONT
POCKET LINING Using 3.25mm needles and col B, cast on 30 sts. Work 3½ in. in st st, then leave on a st holder. Make 2. Using 3.25mm needles and col B, cast on 71 sts and knit 1 row. Work 16 rows in afghan stitch as follows:

ROW 1 (RS) Using col C, k9, ssk, *k17, (sl2, k1, p2sso), rep from * to last 20 sts, k17, k2tog, k1.

ROW 2 Using col C, k1, *p1, k8, (k1, yo, k1) in next st, k8, rep from * to last 10 sts, p1, k9.

ROWS 3 AND 4 Using col B, rep rows 1 and 2.

WAISTCOAT CHART 1: BACK AND FRONTS

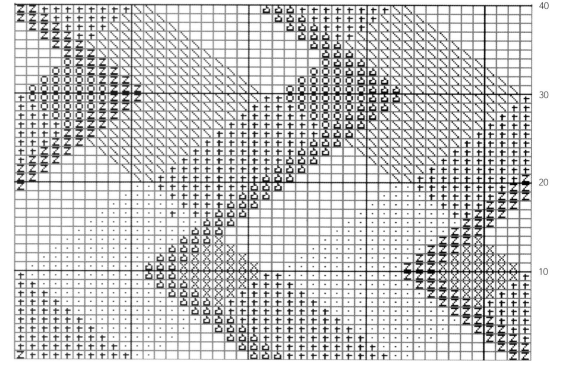

When 16 rows are completed, foll chart 1 and rep the 44 sts across rows as follows:

ROW 1 (RS) Work the last 22 sts, work the 44 sts once, work the first 5 sts (71 sts).

ROW 2 Work the last 5 sts, work the 44 sts once, work the first 22 sts.
Rep the 40 rows of the chart throughout front, inc 1 st at end (outside edge) of every sixth row until there are 84 sts.
At the same time, when work measures 6 in. from cast-on edge and ends on WS, work pocket. Work 23 sts, then place the next 30 sts on a st holder. With RS facing, cont in patt across the 30 sts of pocket lining, then work to end of row. Cont in patt as set until work measures 12 in. from cast-on edge and ends with a RS row.

SHAPE ARMHOLE AND NECKLINE Cast off 7 sts at beg of next row, work to last 2 sts, k2tog. Dec 1 st at armhole edge on next and every row 23 times.

At the same time, shape neck by dec 1 st at neck edge every fifth row 20 times, keeping patt correct as set. Cont until work measures 22½ in. from cast-on edge and ends with a RS row.

SHAPE SHOULDER Cast off 11 sts at beg of next row. Work 1 row. Cast off 11 sts at beg of next row. Work 1 row. Cast of rem 12 sts.

LEFT FRONT

Work as for right front, rev all shapings. Work afghan stitch as follows:

ROW 1 Using col C, k1, ssk, *k17, (sl2, k1, p2sso), rep from * to last 28 sts, k17, k2tog, k9.

ROW 2 Using col C, k9, *p1, k8, (k1, yo, k1) in next st, k8, rep from * to last 2 sts, p1, k1.

ROWS 3 AND 4 Using col B, rep rows 1 and 2.

FINISHING

Join shoulder seams using a small, neat back-stitch on edge of work.

ARMHOLE EDGINGS   With RS facing and using 2.75mm circular needles and col G, pick up and knit 156 sts evenly around armhole edge. Starting on a purl row (reading chart from left to right), work the 5 rows of chart 2 at right, rep the patt across row.

ROWS 6 AND 7   Knit in col G to form fold for hem. Cont in col G and st st, beg on a knit row and work 6 rows. Cast off.

POCKET TOPS   With RS facing and using 2.75mm needles, place sts from st holder onto LH needle and cont in patt from chart 1 for 5 rows. Change to col B and purl 1 row.

NEXT ROW (RS)   Purl in col B to form fold for hem. Using col B and beg with a purl row, work 6 rows in st st. Cast off evenly.

FRONT BAND (WORKED IN ONE PIECE)   With RS facing and using a 2.75mm circular needle and col G, pick up and knit 84 sts along right front to beg of neck shaping; 80 sts along neck shaping to shoulder; 3 sts down back neck; 35 sts from st holder at center back; 3 sts up other side back neck edge; 80 sts down left front neck edge; and 84 sts down left front (369 sts).
Working back and forth and beg with a purl row, work 5 rows of chart 2 as follows:

ROW 1 (WS)   Work 6 sts 61 times across row, work first 3 sts.

ROW 2   Work last 3 sts, work 6 sts 61 times across row.
At the same time, work buttonholes on row 1 as follows:

ROW 1   Work 286 sts, (cast off 3 sts purlwise, p16) 4 times, cast off 3 sts purlwise, p4.

ROW 2   Patt as set, casting on 3 sts across those cast off on previous row.

WAISTCOAT CHART 2: ARMHOLE EDGING AND FRONT BAND

Cont in patt as set until row 5 is completed, then knit 2 rows in col G to form foldline. Beg with a knit row, work 6 rows in col G in st st, working buttonholes on rows 5 and 6 to correspond with those already worked as follows:

ROW 5 (RS)   Work 4 sts, (cast off 3 sts, k16) 4 times, cast off 3 sts, k286.

ROW 6   Patt as set, casting on 3 sts across those cast off on previous row. Cast off evenly. Join side seams using a small, neat backstitch on edge of work, and join afghan stitch with an invisible slipstitch. Turn armhole edgings and front band to WS and slipstitch neatly in place. Fold down pocket tops to WS and slipstitch in place. Sew pocket lining and side edges of tops of pockets in place. Sew together 2 sides of buttonholes. Attach 5 buttons, making sure that the patt is in line across the waistcoat.

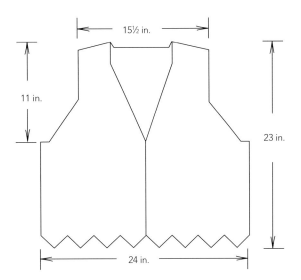

YARN

Rowan Magpie Aran

Key		Colorway 1	Quantity	Colorway 2	Quantity	
□	A	Camel 676	17 hanks	Porridge 771	17 hanks	x 100g
⊙	B	Comanche 503	4 hanks	Squirrel 772	4 hanks	x 100g
⊻	C	Ginger 505	1 hank	Dapple 450	2 hanks	x 100g
⊠	D	Butter 675	1 hank	Squirrel 772		x 100g
⊟	E	Neptune 612	1 hank	Dapple 450		x 100g
⑤	F	Ember 763	1 hank	Dapple 450		x 100g
◪	G	Ivy 765	1 hank	Squirrel 772		x 100g
⊠	H	Squirrel 772	1 hank	Dapple 450		x 100g
⊞	I	Sea Lord 608	1 hank	Squirrel 772		x 100g

T H R O W

NEEDLES

- 4.5mm (USA 7) long-length circular
- Cable needle

TENSION

18 sts and 24 rows = 4 in. or 10cm over patt

MEASUREMENTS

80 in. by 58½ in.

AFGHAN STITCH

Row 1 (RS)   Using col A, k1, ssk, *k13, (sl2-k1-p2sso), rep from * to last 16 sts, k13, k2tog, k1.

Row 2   Using col A, k1, *p1, k6, (k1, yo, k1) in next st, k6, rep from * to last 2 sts, p1, k1.

Rows 3 and 4   Using col B, rep rows 1 and 2.

KNITTING THE THROW

Using col B, cast on 263 sts and knit 1 row. Using afghan stitch and working back and forth, work 40 rows. Knit 1 row in col A. Foll charts 1, 2, and 3 at left and below, work the 56 rows 7 times, then work the first 16 rows (408 rows) as follows (note that charts 1, 2, and 3 start on a purl row, reading from left to right):

ROW 1   8 sts of chart 1, first 4 sts of chart 1, 39 sts of chart 2, last st of chart 1, (8 sts of chart 1)

THROW CHART 1   **THROW CHART 2**

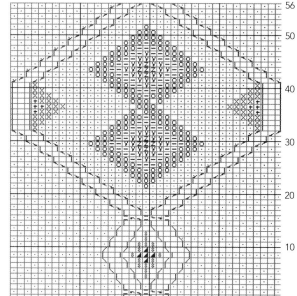

THROW CHART 3

3 times, last 4 sts of chart 1, 103 sts of chart 3, last st of chart 1 (8 sts of chart 1) 3 times, first 4 sts of chart 1, 39 sts of chart 2, last st of chart 1, 8 sts of chart 1, first 3 sts of chart 1 (263 sts). Work 408 rows in patt as set by row 1. Purl 1 row in col A. Work a further 40 rows in afghan stitch, rev the cols, starting with col B and finishing with col A. Using col B, knit 1 row and cast off.

FINISHING

Sew or knit in all ends securely and neatly so the WS of throw is as attractive as possible.

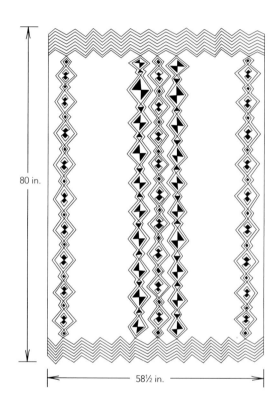

80 in.

58½ in.

Shoowa throw in colorway 2 (left)
and colorway 1

THROW STITCH KEY

⊡   rev st st—purl on RS and knit on WS

3 over 3 cross (over 7 sts)—sl 4 sts to cn and hold at front, k3, sl the center st from cn back to LH needle and purl it, then k3 from cn

3 over 3 cross (over 7 sts)—sl 4 sts to cn and hold at back, k3, sl the center st from cn back to LH needle and purl it, then k3 from cn

3 over 1 cross (over 4 sts)—sl 3 sts to cn and hold at front, p1, then k3 from cn

3 over 1 cross (over 4 sts)—sl 1 st to cn and hold at back, k3, then p1 from cn

3 over 2 cross (over 5 sts)—sl 3 sts to cn and hold at front, p2, then k3 from cn

3 over 2 cross (over 5 sts)—sl 2 sts to cn and hold at back, k3, then p2 from cn

Note: All the cable crossings occur on knit rows as chart starts on purl row (reading from left to right)

HAT

NEEDLES
- 3.25mm (USA 4) circular
- 3.75mm (USA 5) circular
- Set of four double-pointed 3.75mm (USA 5)
- Cable needle

TENSION
25 sts and 32 rows = 4 in. or 10cm over st st

MEASUREMENTS
22-in. circumference

INTARSIA KNITTING
Because the hat is knitted in the round, the yarn will be at the WS of each color block at the end of every round. Loosely strand the yarn back to the beginning of its color block, making sure that enough yarn is left on the WS so as not to pull the work in. Cut and tidy before the facing is turned up.

YARN
Rowan Lightweight DK

Key		Colorway 1	Colorway 2	Quantity	
□	A	Charcoal 625	Black 62	4 hanks	x 25g
X	B	Petrol Blue 54	Teal Green 91	1 hank	x 25g
O	C	Ginger 27	Blue 56	1 hank	x 25g
+	D	Slate 53	Claret 46	1 hank	x 25g
△	E	Red 46	Old Gold 9	1 hank	x 25g
*	F	Sunshine 426	Rust 77	1 hank	x 25g
⋈	G	Green 91	Purple 99	1 hank	x 25g

KNITTING THE HAT
Using 3.25mm circular needle and col A, cast on 130 sts. Working in the round, work 6 in. in k1, p1 rib. Purl 1 rnd to form foldline, inc 5 sts evenly around (135 sts). Knit 1 rnd. Change to 3.75mm circular needle and mark end of last rnd. Foll chart 1 below and working in st st, work rnds 1 to 6 inclusive, all rows being knit rows.

NEXT ROW   Make a small tuck on outside of work by working sts on this row as follows: Using col A, put needle in front of st as if to knit, then put needle through first loop on marked row (last row before chart) and knit the two together. Rep this around to form a tuck on RS.
Knit a further 3 rnds in col A, marking both ends of last rnd as before. Foll chart 1, work rnds 7 to 12 inclusive. Make a tuck as before on next rnd. Knit a further 3 rnds in col A, marking both ends of last round. Foll chart 1, work rnds 13 to 18 inclusive. Make a tuck as before on next rnd. Foll chart 2 on the facing page, rep the 27 sts 5 times around (all rows are knit rows). When the 38 rnds are completed, mark both ends of the final rnd. Foll chart 1, work rnds 7 to 12 inclusive and make another tuck as before. Knit 1 row in col A, dec 1 st every 44 sts 3 times (132 sts).

HAT CHART 1

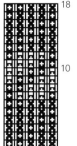

HAT STITCH KEY

 Using col A, rev st st—purl on RS rows and knit on WS

 Using col G, 2 over 2 cross (over 5 sts)—sl 3 sts to cn and hold at front, k2, sl the center st from cn back to LH needle and knit it in the color of the symbol above it, then k2 from cn

\\ Using col G, 2 over 1 cross (over 3 sts)—sl 2 sts to cn and hold at front, k1 in the color of the next symbol on the row, then k2 from cn

// Using col G, 2 over 1 cross (over 3 sts)—sl 1 st to cn and hold at back, k2, then k1 from cn in the col of the next symbol on the row

Using col G, 2 over 2 cross (over 4 sts)—sl 2 sts to cn and hold at front, k2, then k2 from cn

SHAPE CROWN Using double-pointed 3.75mm needles and col A, place 44 sts on each of 3 needles and beg knitting with the fourth needle. Foll chart 3 at right for crown. Foll the 22-st rep patt as follows:

RND 1 *Sl1, ssk, k16, k2tog, k1, rep from * to end.

RND 2 Knit.
Rep these 2 rnds, progressively substituting k14, k12, k10, k8, k6, k4, k2, k1 for k16 on subsequent repeats. Cont for 18 rnds until there are 24 sts.

NEXT ROW K2tog on every st (12 sts). Break yarn, leaving 10 in., and thread through all sts. Fasten off securely on WS.

FINISHING
Turn facing (k1, p1 rib in col A) onto WS and hem neatly along inside of tuck at crown.

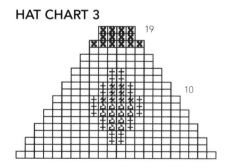

Shoowa hats in colorway 2 (left) and colorway 1

HAT CHART 2

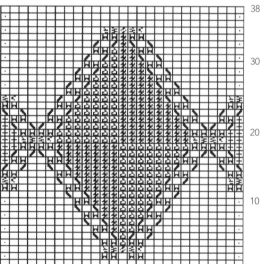

38
30
20
10

HAT CHART 3

19
10

KUBA

TUNIC

CARDIGAN

PILLOW

SOCKS

Over the past few years, the cut-pile raffia embroideries from the kingdom of Kuba, in what is now Congo, have been so influential in my designs that I feel I have to include them in two chapters. The checkerboard is widely used in decorative art and symbolizes the two halves of a whole—day and night, birth and death, young and old, health and illness, success and failure, female and male. The checkerboard is a reminder of the natural rhythms and cycles of the universe, of how life is a combination of positive and negative influences, and of the importance of trying to maintain a balance between the two.

I love the way that checks and chevrons are juxtaposed in Kuba patterns, and I've developed this idea in these four pieces. In the Kuba tunic and cardigan, I use one of my favorite design ploys: repeating a motif from the sweater in the ribs. The checker-board-striped ribs create a coherent visual impact, underlining the importance of the checks in the overall design scheme.

Knitting is full of surprises. When I first incorporated motifs and stitch patterns into my ribs, I discovered that this produces a variety of interesting scalloped edges as a bonus. In the tunic, I use the checks and chevrons to frame the back and front by repeating them up the center of the sleeve into the saddle shoulder to the neckband. The checkered diamond in the cardigan is emphasized by the wonderful black and white buttons. In the Kuba pillow, I have introduced texture by punctuating the design with a sculptured checkerboard stitch in the main color, and I have framed the pillow with handmade three-colored woolen cord. The Kuba socks are finished with an intriguing braid pattern that creates the illusion of the socks having been knitted sideways.

These four Kuba designs are not for novice knitters, but a moderately experienced intarsia knitter can tackle the tunic and cardigan with confidence, and any competent Fair Isle knitter can knit the pillow and socks.

TUNIC

NEEDLES

Cotton version:
- 3.25mm (USA 3)
- 3.75mm (USA 5)
- 3.25mm (USA 3) circular

Wool version:
- 3.25mm (USA 3)
- 4mm (USA 6)
- 3.25mm (USA 3) circular

TENSION

24 sts and 30 rows = 4 in. or 10cm over intarsia patt

SIZE

One size to fit 34-in. to 44-in. bust
See diagram on p. 29 for finished knitted measurements.

YARN

Rowan Cotton Glace (cotton version); Rowan Lightweight DK (wool version)

	Key		Color	Quantity	
Cotton version	☐	A	Oyster 730	11 balls	x 50g
	☒	B	Provence 744	3 balls	x 50g
	⊡	C	Dusk 439	3 balls	x 50g
	⊘	D	Adobe 434	2 balls	x 50g
	⊠	E	Dijon 739	1 ball	x 50g
	☑	F	Air Force 442	3 balls	x 50g
	⊞	G	Blood Orange 445	4 balls	x 50g
Wool version	☐	A	Chocolate 80	16 hanks	x 25g
	☒	B	Green 91	4 hanks	x 25g
	⊡	C	Cinnamon 81	4 hanks	x 25g
	⊘	D	Teal Blue 54	2 hanks	x 25g
	⊠	E	Old Gold 9	2 hanks	x 25g
	☑	F	Rust 27	4 hanks	x 25g
	⊞	G	Burgundy 663	7 hanks	x 25g

Previous page: Kuba cardigan (left) and tunic in cotton

TUNIC CHART 1: RIBS AND NECKBAND

BACK AND FRONT

Using 3.25mm needles and col G, cast on 154 sts. Foll chart 1 below, work the first 22 rows for rib as follows (note that col G can be stranded loosely across checkerboard patt, which should be knitted intarsia):

ROW 1 Work the 16 sts of chart 9 times across row, work the first 10 sts.

ROW 2 Work the last 10 sts of chart, work the 16 sts of chart 9 times across row.
Rep the 4 rows of chart until 20 rows have been worked, then work the first 2 rows (22 rows). Change to 4mm needles. Foll chart 2 on the facing page, work the 174 rows.

ARMHOLE SHAPING: ROW 115 K2, sl1, k1, psso, work to last 4 sts, k2tog, k2.
Cont dec in this way every alt row until there are 132 sts. Start neck shaping on row 170, leaving center 32 sts on a st holder. Foll chart 2 to row 174 and cast off.

SLEEVES

Using 3.25mm needles and col G, cast on 50 sts. Foll chart 1 below, work the first 22 rows for rib as follows:

ROW 1
Work the last 12 sts of chart, work the 16 sts twice across row, work the first 6 sts (50 sts).

ROW 2
Work the last 6 sts, work the 16 sts twice, work the first 12 sts.
Change to 4mm needles. Foll chart 3 on p. 28, work the 112 rows, inc 1 st at both ends of first and every alt row 6 times (62 sts), and then every third row 31 times (124 sts).

ROW 112 Cast off 49 sts. Work to end.

ROW 113 Cast off 49 sts. Work to end.
Cont on rem 26 sts, keeping patt correct to row 168, then place sts on a st holder.

NECKBAND

Using a circular 3.25mm needle and col G, with RS facing, pick up and knit 26 sts from st holder at left sleeve; 3 sts down center front; 32 sts across center front; 3 sts up other side of center front; 26 sts from st holder at right sleeve; 3 sts down back neck; 32 sts across center back neck; and 3 sts up other side of back neck (128 sts). Purl 1 row. Then working back and forth (not in

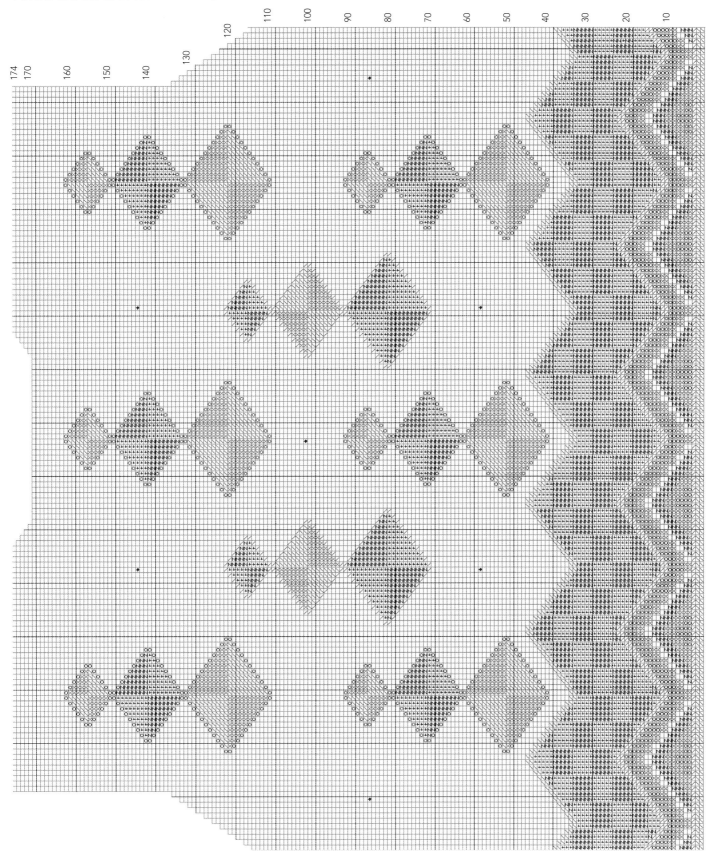

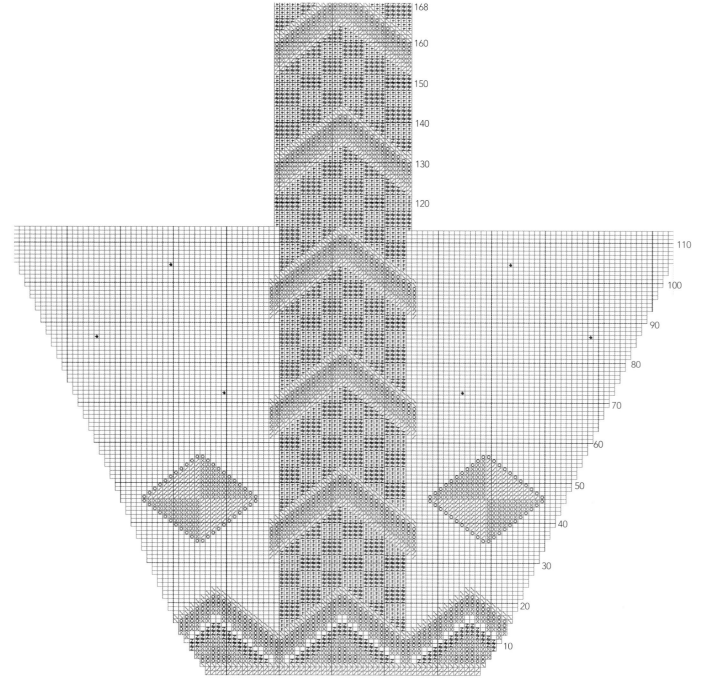

TUNIC STITCH KEY

⊡ Rev st st—purl on RS rows and knit on WS rows in col G

◆ Make small bobble in col A—knit into this st without slipping it off the needle, bring yarn forward, knit again into the same st, and sl it off the needle. Turn the work and purl the 3 made sts. Turn the work and knit the 3 made sts. Turn the work, purl 2 sts tog, purl 1 st. Turn the work, sl 1 st, knit 1 st, pass slipped st over the knit st to complete the bobble.

the round), foll chart 1 on p. 26 and rep the 16 sts across row 8 times, working from right to left on RS rows and from left to right on WS rows.
Note: Weave in col G behind the checkerboard patt, which should be knitted intarsia.
Cont until neckband measures 2½ in., then cast off in col G.

FINISHING

Use a small, neat backstitch on edge of work for all seams. Join shoulder seams of back and front to side edges of saddle on sleeves. Sew cast-off edge of sleeves to armhole edge of sweater (including the decreased edge) on both sides of the shoulder. Join side and sleeve seams in one line from top of rib to top of rib. Join ribs and neckband with an invisible slipstitch so that they lie flat.

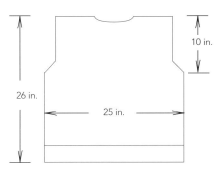

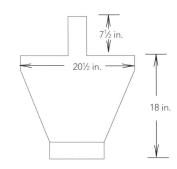

Kuba tunic in wool

CARDIGAN

NEEDLES
- 3mm (USA 2)
- 3.75mm (USA 5)
- 3mm (USA 2) circular

BUTTONS
Six 16mm

TENSION
24 sts and 32 rows = 4 in. or 10cm over intarsia patt

SIZE
One size to fit 34-in. to 42-in. bust
See diagram on p. 34 for finished knitted measurements.

YARN
Rowan Cotton Glace

Key		Colorway 1	Colorway 2	Quantity	
□	A	Swimming Pool 438	Blood Orange 445	11 balls	x 50g
X	B	Blood Orange 445	Swimming Pool 438	2 balls	x 50g
O	C	Banana 444	Banana 444	2 balls	x 50g
⁄	D	Black 727	Black 727	2 balls	x 50g
\	E	Dusk 439	Air Force 442	2 balls	x 50g
Z	F	Air Force 442	Adobe 434	3 balls	x 50g
+	G	Oyster 730	Oyster 730	2 balls	x 50g

CARDIGAN STITCH KEY

·	rev st st—purl on RS and knit on WS in col F

BACK
Using 3mm needles and col F, cast on 140 sts. Foll chart 1 on p. 32, work the 10 rows of rib. Change to 3.75mm needles and cont to work from chart until row 92 is completed.

SHAPE ARMHOLE: ROW 93   Cast off 10 sts at beg of row. Work to end.

ROW 94   Cast off 10 sts at beg of row. Work to end (120 sts).
Cont working from chart until row 164 is completed.

SHAPE SHOULDERS AND NECKLINE: ROW 165
Cast off 14 sts at beg of row, work 30 sts, turn, and leave rem sts on a st holder. Work each side separately.

ROW 166   Dec 1 st at beg of row. Work to end.

ROW 167   Cast off 14 sts, work to last 2 sts, k2tog.

ROW 168   P2tog. Work to end.

ROW 169   Cast off rem 14 sts.
With RS facing, rejoin yarn to rem sts and cast off center 30 sts, patt to end. Complete to match other side, rev all shapings.

LEFT FRONT
Using 3mm needles and col F, cast on 69 sts. Foll chart 1 on p. 32, work the 10 rows of rib. Change to 3.75mm needles and cont in patt from chart for left front until row 92 is completed.

SHAPE ARMHOLE   Cast off 10 sts at beg of next row, patt to end. Cont until row 96 is completed.

SHAPE NECKLINE   Dec 1 st at neck edge on next and every foll third row 3 times (56 sts), then every foll fourth row 14 times (42 sts). Cont in patt until row 164 is completed.

SHAPE SHOULDER: ROW 165   Cast off 14 sts at beg, patt to end.

ROW 166   Work as per chart 1.

ROW 167   Cast off 14 sts at beg, patt to end.

ROW 168   Work as per chart 1.

ROW 169   Cast off rem 14 sts.

Kuba cardigan in colorway 1

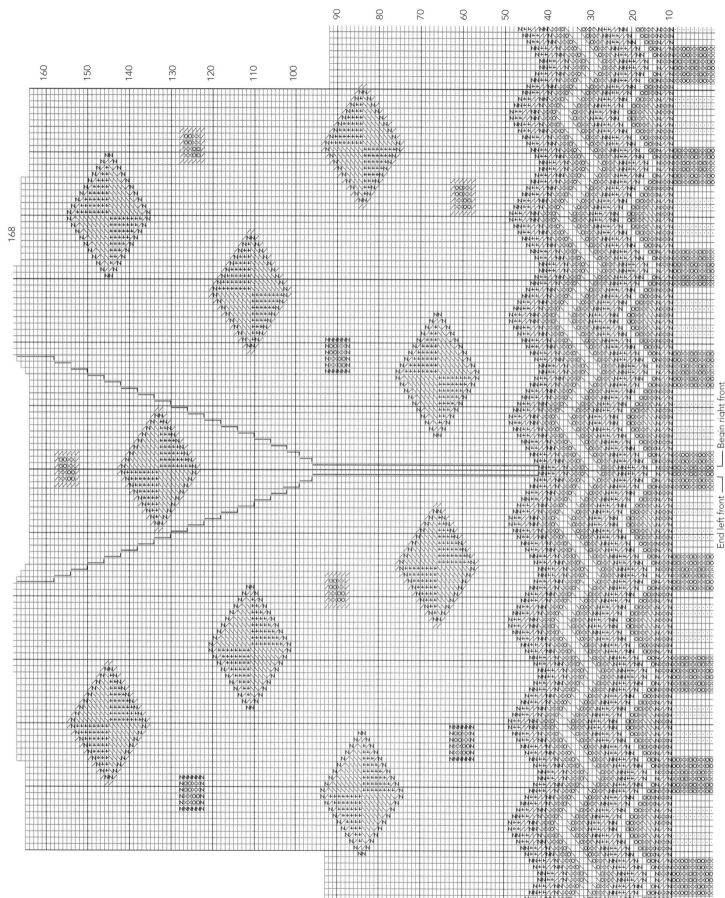

CARDIGAN CHART 2: SLEEVE

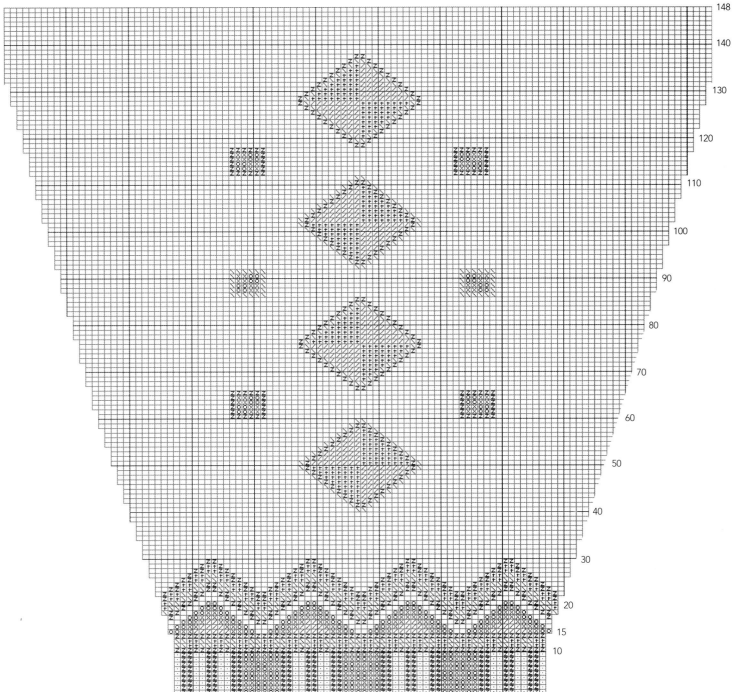

148
140
130
120
110
100
90
80
70
60
50
40
30
20
15
10

RIGHT FRONT

Foll chart 1 as for left front but rev all shapings.

SLEEVES

Using 3mm needles and col F, cast on 60 sts. Foll chart 2 above, work the 10 rows of rib. Change to 3.75mm needles and cont to foll chart, inc 1 st at both ends of row 15 and every foll fourth row 13 times (86 sts), then every fifth

row 14 times (114 sts). Cont to foll chart until 148 rows are completed. Cast off.

FRONT BAND (KNITTED IN ONE PIECE)

Join both shoulder seams using a small, neat backstitch on edge of work.
With RS facing and using col B and a 3mm circular needle (but working back and forth, not in the round), pick up and knit 78 sts up right front to beg of neck shaping; 66 sts up neckline

CARDIGAN CHART 3: FRONT BAND

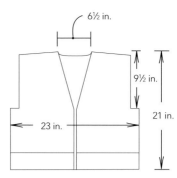

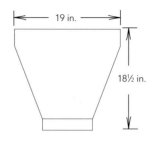

to shoulder; 42 sts from st holder at back neck; 66 sts down sloping edge of left front neck; and 78 sts down left front to cast-on edge (330 sts). Mark the 76th st up from bottom of right front for start of buttonholes.

Joining in col C, work 6 rows in patt from chart 3 on p. 33 as follows:

ROW 1 (WS) P2 in col B, *p2 in col C, p2 in col B, rep from * to end.

ROW 2 K2 in col B, *k2 in col C, k2 in col B, rep from * to end.

At the same time, work buttonholes as follows: Patt 3 sts, *cast off 3 sts, patt 11 sts, rep from * 4 times, cast off 3 sts, patt to end. The sixth buttonhole should bring you to marker.

Work 4 more rows in patt from chart 3, casting on the 3 sts over those cast off when you come to them on next row.

NEXT ROW (WS) Using col F, purl.

NEXT ROW (RS) Using col F, purl to form fold-line. Work 7 rows in k1, p1 rib in col F, working buttonholes on rows 5 and 6 to correspond with those worked previously. Cast off loosely.

FINISHING

Fold front band to WS at foldline and slipstitch in place. Neatly stitch 2 sides of each buttonhole together.

Use a small, neat backstitch for all seams, matching patterns carefully. For ribs, use an invisible edge-to-edge stitch so the ribs lie flat. Insert sleeves, placing the cast-off edge along vertical edge of armhole. Three-quarters of the vertical straight edge of sleeve lies along cast-off edge of armhole. Join side and sleeve seams in one line.

Sew 6 buttons onto left front band directly opposite buttonholes, making sure that the patt is in line across front of cardigan.

YARN

Rowan Designer DK

Key		Colorway 1	Colorway 2	Quantity	
☐	A	Mocha 698	Slate 065	3 balls	x 50g
⌀	B	Cinnamon 691	Teal 685	2 balls	x 50g
Ⓞ	C	Old Gold 690	Old Gold 690	1 ball	x 50g
Ⓥ	D	Taupe 695	Steel 697	2 balls	x 50g
⊞	E	Burgundy 659	Cinnamon 691	1 ball	x 50g
Ⓩ	F	Lemon 623	Mocha 698	1 ball	x 50g
⊟	G	Rust 663	Turquoise 661	1 ball	x 50g

PILLOW

NEEDLES
• 4mm (USA 6)

TENSION
24 sts and 32 rows = 4 in. or 10cm over patt

MEASUREMENTS
30 in. by 13½ in.

BACK
Using col A, cast on 84 sts. Foll chart 1 below, work 16 rows, rep the 4 rows 4 times as follows:

ROW 1 (WS) Rep the 12 sts of chart 1 across row 7 times.

ROW 2 Rep the 12 sts of chart 1 across row 7 times.

Purl 1 row. Foll chart 2 on the facing page, work the 48 rows, rep the 12 sts as before 7 times across rows. Cont in col A , knit 1 row. Foll chart 1, work 24 rows in col A. Purl 1 row in col A. Foll chart 3 on the facing page, work the 64 rows, rep the 12 sts as before across rows. Knit 1 row in col A. Foll chart 1, work another 24 rows in col A. Purl 1 row in col A. Foll chart 2, work the 48 rows. Knit 1 row in col A. Foll chart 1, work a final 16 rows in col A. Cast off.

FRONT
Work as for back to end, then cont in col A and purl 2 rows to form foldline for hem. Cont in chart 1 for a further 28 rows. Cast off.

FINISHING
Use a small, neat backstitch on edge of work for all seams. Turn down extra 3½ in. of front on inside and oversew in place down side seams (do not sew the hem across width of pillow). With right sides of pillow facing, sew around three sides, leaving top end open, with extra 3½ in. turned down. Make or buy rope to match, then attach, making loops at corners if preferred.

PILLOW CHART 1

PILLOW CHART 3

Kuba pillow in colorway 1 (front) and colorway 2 (back)

PILLOW CHART 2

PILLOW STITCH KEY

☐ rev st st—purl on RS and knit on

WS in col A

SOCKS

NEEDLES

- Set of four double-pointed 4mm (USA 6)
- Tapestry needle

TENSION

24 sts and 30 rows = 4 in. or 10cm over patt

MEASUREMENTS

To fit U.S. shoe sizes 5½ to 8½ (English sizes 4 to 7)

YARN

Rowan Designer DK (cols A, B, D, E); Rowan Kid Silk (col C)

Key		Colorway 1	Colorway 2	Quantity	
☐	A	Natural 649	Black 062	1 ball	x 50g
☒	B	Rust 663	Rust 663	1 ball	x 50g
Ⓞ	C	Old Gold 989	Old Gold 989	1 ball	x 25g
▨	D	Black 062	Camel 693	1 ball	x 50g
⊞	E	Teal Green 661	Red 632	1 ball	x 50g

LEG

Cast on 44 sts with col A over the index finger and col B over the thumb using the continental method (see p. 8).

Make a loop using both cols (loop does not figure in the total st count). When all sts have been cast on, remove the loop. Divide the sts evenly onto 3 needles. Join into a rnd, being careful not to twist sts. This join marks the seam-line and beg of the rnd.

BRAID PATTERN: RND 1 *K1 col A, k1 col B, rep from * around.

RND 2 Bring both cols to the front of the work. Keep them in the same order as on the previous rnd. *P1 col A, p1 col B, always bringing the next col to be used *over* the top of the last col used. Rep from * around.

RND 3 *P1 col A, p1 col B, always bringing the next col to be used *under* the last col used. Rep from * around.

Rep these 3 rnds one more time, inc 1 st at both ends of last row. Beg foll the chart on the facing page, inc 1 st at both ends of first row (48 sts after row 1). Work every rnd, working the 8 sts of

Kuba socks in colorway 2 (left) and colorway 1

chart 6 times around. (Note: As all rnds are knit rnds, chart is read from right to left on every row.) When the 33 rows of chart are completed, cont to rep rows 24 to 33 inclusive for rest of sock. When a further 5 rnds have been worked, break both yarns and divide for heel. Place the first 11 sts and the last 12 sts of the rnd onto one needle for heel. Place the rem 25 sts onto another needle for the instep.

HEEL

ROW 1 With RS facing, join col A and col B. Working over the 23 sts, *k1 col A, k1 col B. Rep from *, ending k1 col A. Turn.

ROW 2 *P1 col A, p1 col B. Rep from *, ending p1 col A. Turn.
Rep these last 2 rows 7 more times for a total of 16 rows, then turn heel. (K1 col A, k1 col B) 7 times, k1 col A, k2tog tbl with col B, turn. *Sl1 as to purl, (p1 col A, p1 col B) 3 times, p1 col A, p2tog with col B, turn. Sl1 as to purl, (k1 col A, k1 col B) 3 times, k1 col A, k2tog tbl with col B. Turn. Rep from * until all sts are worked. When you have 9 heels sts, end ready to begin a RS row.

GUSSETS

On needle 1, work across 9 heel sts as follows: sl1, k4 col D, k4 col E. With col D, pick up and k12 along right side of heel flap. On needle 2, work across the 25 instep sts in checkerboard patt as set, foll the 10-row rep of chart. Pick up and k1 to make 26 sts on needle 2. On needle 3 with col E, pick up and k11 along left side of heel flap, then slip first 5 sts from needle 1 onto needle 3. There are 16 sts on needle 1, 26 sts on needle 2, and 16 sts on needle 3.

SHAPE GUSSETS: RND 1 Needle 1: k4 col E, k4 col D, k4 col E, k1 col D, k2tog col D, k1 col D.
Needle 2: ssk col D, k3 col D, k4 col E, k4 col D, k4 col E, k4 col D, k3 col E, k2tog col E.
Needle 3: k1 col E, ssk col E, k1 col E, k4 col D, k4 col E, k4 col D.

RND 2 Work in checkerboard patt as set.

RND 3 Needle 1: k4 col E, k4 col D, k4 col E, k2tog col D, k1 col D.
Needle 2: (k4 col D, k4 col E) 3 times.
Needle 3: k1 col E, ssk col E, k4 col D, k4 col E, k4 col D.

RND 4 Work in checkerboard patt as set.
Cont in this manner, foll the checkerboard patt. Meanwhile, (k2tog, k1 at the end of needle 1, and k1, ssk at beg of needle 3) every patt rnd 2 more times. There are now 12 sts on needles 1 and 3 and 24 sts on needle 2.
Cont in checkerboard patt as set until foot length measures 6 in. from end of heel shaping or approx 8 in. overall. Lengthen or shorten here as desired. End at top of set of 5-row checkerboard rep.

SHAPE TOE

RND 1 Using col B, knit to 3 sts from the end of needle 1, k2tog, k1. K1, ssk at beg of needle 2 and work to 3 sts from the end of needle 2, k2tog, k1. K1, ssk at beg of needle 3. Work to end of rnd.

RND 2 Knit with col A.
Rep these last two rnds until there are 6 sts on needles 1 and 3 and 12 sts on needle 2. Cont in striped patt, work rnd 1 (the dec rnd) until there are 2 sts on needles 1 and 3 and 4 sts on needle 2. Break the yarn, leaving a 10-in. tail. Thread the tail through a tapestry needle and draw through the rem sts. Tighten up to finish the toe.

FINISHING

Weave in the ends neatly and securely.

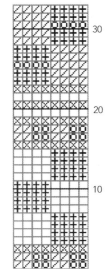

BALUCH

JACKET

SWEATER

PILLOW

SOCKS

The ubiquitous eight-pointed star has been a recurring theme in my work. Known either as the Star of Solomon or the Jewel of Muhammed, it figures prominently in world textiles but especially in Turkish and Caucasian weaving. The nomadic Baluchi, living in the mountains of Afghanistan and Iran, have imported the star into their work, as you can see above in this tough yet beautiful double-pouched saddlebag.

Recognizable by their lustrous, high-quality wool dyed in rich, dark aubergine, claret, green, indigo, umber, and black, Baluch textiles have assimilated design elements from many other Middle Eastern traditions.

I love the idea of such a visual melting pot, so I have mixed the jewel colors and stars from the saddlebag with a variety of textured stitches. In the Baluch jacket, the stars surround a vertical stripe of sculptured knots. This design not only satisfies my passion for combining texture and color but also incorporates another of my favorite ideas by breaking up the

vertical lines with horizontal bands of pattern. If you prefer, the button bands can be worked in solid moss stitch as in color-way 2. In the Baluch sweater, the star is framed by the sculptured trellis, which develops into the stained-glass diamonds at the corners. This is another favorite design, and it works just as beautifully without the star. The trellis is repeated at the hem, cuffs, and collar in the reversible lacy border.

In the Baluch pillow, I have used chenille yarn to achieve the sumptuously colorful star and border. The back of the pillow repeats the star border in an allover textured stitch, picking out just one colored star at the center. Eastern sock construction is used in the Baluch socks, which can be knitted either flat or in the round. Although intarsia is quite fussy in the round, I think the beautiful seamless finish more than justifies the patience it demands. The large stars are framed by astral braiding and finished with a firmament of stars on the sole.

Baluch jacket in colorway 2 (left) and colorway 1

YARN

Rowan DK Cotton

Key		Colorway 1	Colorway 2	Quantity	
□	A	Sea Green 237	Port 245	17 balls	x 50g
△	B	Port 245	Evergreen 238	2 balls	x 50g
O	C	Royal 294	Sailor Blue 232	2 balls	x 50g
⊞	D	Green 219	Azure 248	1 ball	x 50g
◢	E	Damson 226	Olive 247	2 balls	x 50g
Z	F	Azure 248	Scarlet 255	1 ball	x 50g
−	G	Olive 247	Sea Green 237	2 balls	x 50g
⊙	H	Red 215	Sunkissed 231	1 ball	x 50g

Previous page: Baluch socks in colorway 1, jacket in colorway 1, and pillow in colorway 2

JACKET

NEEDLES

- 3.25mm (USA 3)
- 4mm (USA 6)
- Cable needle

BUTTONS

Six 20mm

TENSION

24 sts and 30 rows = 4 in. or 10cm over patt

SIZE

One size to fit 34-in. to 42-in. bust
See diagram on p. 43 for finished knitted
measurements.

BACK

Using 3.25mm needles and col A, cast on
131 sts and work 10 rows in st st. Purl 2 rows to
form foldline for hem. Foll chart below, work the
first 12 rows.

JACKET CHART

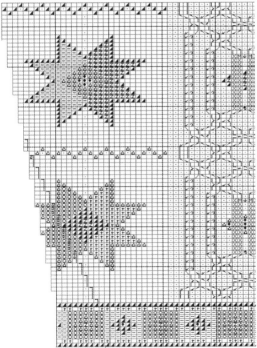

End sleeve

JACKET STITCH KEY

·   rev st st in col A—purl on RS and knit on WS

bind 2—yarn over, p2, pass yarn over

X   no st

M   make 1

double inc—work (k1b, k1) into same st, then insert tip of LH needle behind vertical strand that runs downward between the two sts just made, and k1b into this strand to make the third st of the group

work 5 sts together—sl 3 sts with yarn in front, drop yarn, then *pass second st on RH needle over the first and off the needle (center st of dec), sl center st back to LH needle and pass second st on LH needle over it*, sl the center st back to RH needle again and rep from * to *, then pick up yarn and work the center st

sl 2 sts to cn and hold in back, k2, then k2 from cn

sl 2 sts to cn and hold at front, k2, then k2 from cn

sl 3 sts to cn and hold at front, k2, then sl the center st from cn back to LH needle and purl it, k2 from cn

sl 3 sts to cn and hold at back, k2, then sl the center st from cn back to LH needle and purl it, k2 from cn

sl 1 st to cn and hold at back, k2, then p1 from cn

sl 2 sts to cn and hold at back, k2, then p2 from cn

sl 2 sts to cn and hold at front, p1, then k2 from cn

sl 2 sts to cn and hold at front, p2, then k2 from cn

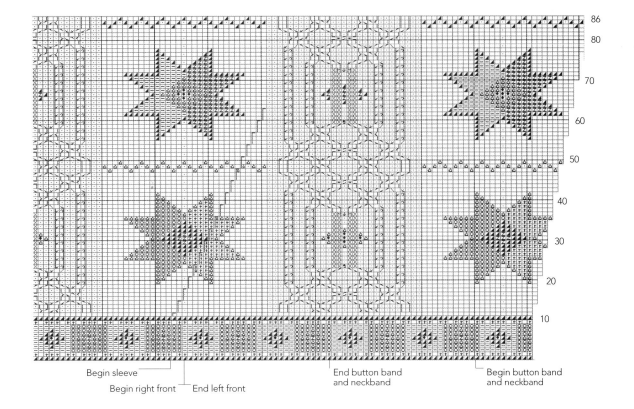

Begin sleeve

Begin right front   End left front

End button band and neckband

Begin button band and neckband

Change to 4mm needles and cont with chart, inc 1 st at both ends of third and every foll seventh row until there are 151 sts. Rep rows 15 to 86 of chart until work measures 12 in. from hemline fold and ends with a WS row.

SHAPE ARMHOLE Keeping patt correct, cast off 3 sts at beg of next 2 rows. Work without shaping until work measures 21½ in. from hemline fold and ends with a WS row.

SHAPE NECKLINE Work the first 58 sts in patt, turn, and leave rem sts on a st holder. Working first side of neck only, dec 1 st at beg of next row (neck edge), then at neck edge on every foll row 4 times in all (54 sts). Sl remainder onto a st holder. Return to rem sts, and with RS facing, sl center 29 sts onto a st holder, rejoin yarn to rem 58 sts, and work in patt to end of row. Complete second side of neck to match first side, rev shaping.

LEFT FRONT

POCKET LINING Using 4mm needles and col A, cast on 25 sts. Beg with a knit row, work 24 rows in st st, ending with a WS row. Break off yarn and sl sts onto a st holder.

BEGIN FRONT Using 3.25mm needles and col A, cast on 66 sts and work 10 rows in st st. Purl 2 rows to form hemline fold. Foll chart and beg on row 1, work sts 1 to 66 inclusive. Foll chart until row 12 has been completed, then change to 4mm needles and cont foll chart, inc 1 st at end (side edge) of third and every foll seventh row until there are 76 sts. **At the same time,** when row 35 has been completed, ending with a RS row, insert pocket lining.

ROW 36 (WS) Work the first 18 sts in patt, sl the next 25 sts onto a st holder, then with RS of pocket lining facing, work in patt across 25 sts of pocket lining and work rem 27 sts in patt. Cont to work from chart, rep rows 15 to 86 throughout until number of rows equals that on back to armhole shaping, ending with a WS row.

ARMHOLE SHAPING Keeping patt correct, cast off 3 sts at beg of next row (73 sts). Cont until work measures 19¼ in. from hemline fold, ending with a RS row.

NECK SHAPING Cast off 7 sts at beg of next row, then dec 1 st at neck edge on next row and every foll row 12 times (54 sts). Cont until number of rows equals that on back to shoulder, ending with a RS row. Sl sts onto a st holder.

RIGHT FRONT

Work as for left front, rev all shapings and working from sts 66 to 131 inclusive on chart.

SLEEVES

Using 3.25mm needles and col A, cast on 55 sts and work 10 rows in st st. Purl 2 rows to form hemline fold. Foll chart, work the first 12 rows over sts 69-123.

Change to 4mm needles and cont with chart, inc 1 st at both ends of next and every foll third row 24 times (103 sts) and then every fourth row 9 times (121 sts), rep patt to top of sleeve.

Note: After the row 63 inc, cont to inc as set, but do not work patt over subsequent inc sts. These sts should be worked in Irish moss st as follows:

ROW 1 *K1, p1, rep from * to end.

ROW 2 *K1, p1, rep from * to end.

ROW 3 *P1, k1, rep from * to end.

ROW 4 *P1, k1, rep from * to end.

These instructions are for an even number of sts. Also keep Irish moss st correct while inc when you have an odd number of sts. When all sts have been inc, cont until work measures 17 in. from hemline fold, keeping Irish moss st and chart patt correct. Cast off firmly.

BUTTON BAND

Press pieces lightly on WS with a warm iron. Using 3.25mm needles and col A, join left shoulder seam by placing WS of back and WS of front tog. With left front facing, knit through both layers along shoulder sts, taking 1 st from left front st holder tog with 1 st from back st holder with each st and casting off as the row is worked. Join right shoulder seam in same way. Use a small, neat backstitch on the edge of work for all seams, matching the notches made by slipping the first st, etc.

Placing center of top of sleeve at shoulder seam, sew cast-off edge of sleeves to vertical armhole edge, cont the seam along cast-off edge of armhole and stitching the latter to the top ½ in. of sleeve. Join side and sleeve seams in one line. Turn hem on back and fronts to WS along purl row and slipstitch in place. Turn hem on sleeves to WS and similarly slipstitch in place.

Using 3.25mm needles and col E with RS facing, pick up and knit 112 sts along left front. The last 8 sts should be over the first 11 rows of border at bottom of front so that squares match up at bottom. Using col E, purl 1 row. Foll chart for button band, rep the 28 sts 4 times across row. Work the 9 rows, then purl 2 rows. Change to col A and work 11 rows in st st, starting with a purl row. Cast off.

Mark positions for 6 buttons, the first ¾ in. from lower edge, the sixth ¾ in. above neck shaping (worked horizontally in neckband), and the rem 4 buttons spaced evenly between.

BUTTONHOLE BAND

Work as for button band along right front. **At the same time,** work buttonholes on row 4 of chart by casting off 3 sts when position of each button is reached, then casting these 3 sts on again on foll row. Work buttonholes similarly over fifth and sixth rows in st st to correspond to first set. Turn front bands to WS along foldline for hem and slipstitch in place.

NECKBAND

Using 3.25mm needles and col E with RS facing, pick up and knit 37 sts evenly up right side front neck; 4 sts down back neck; 29 sts from st holder at center back; 4 sts up back neck; and 38 sts down left front neck edge (112 sts). The first and last 7 sts should be in line with front bands. Using col E, purl 1 row. Foll chart, work the 9 rows. **At the same time,** on row 4 cast off 3 sts (4 sts from edge) above buttonhole band, then cast on these sts on foll row. Purl 2 rows. Change to col A and work 11 rows in st st, working buttonhole to correspond with the previous one on fifth and sixth rows. Cast off loosely in rib.

FINISHING

Turn neckband to WS along hemline fold and slipstitch in place.

POCKET TOPS Using 3.25 needles and col A with RS facing, work 5 rows in single moss st (rows 1 and 3 of Irish moss) across the 25 sts of left front pocket, dec 1 st at both ends of first and third rows (21 sts). Cast off.

Work top of right front pocket similarly. Slipstitch side of pocket tops neatly in place. Slipstitch pocket linings to WS of fronts to end on top of hem. Sew 2 layers of each buttonhole together. Sew buttons onto button band and neckband opposite buttonholes, making sure patt is in line across the jacket.

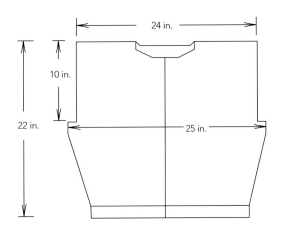

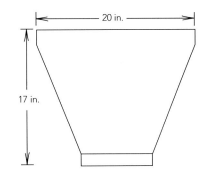

Baluch sweater in colorway 2 (left) and colorway 1

SWEATER

NEEDLES
- 3mm (USA 2)
- 3.25mm (USA 3)
- 3.75mm (USA 5)

TENSION
25 sts and 32 rows = 4 in. or 10cm over main patt

SIZE
One size to fit 32-in. to 38-in. bust
See diagram on p. 47 for finished knitted measurements.

BACK
Using 3.75mm needles and col A, cast on 136 sts. Foll chart on the facing page, work in st st until row 64 is completed.

SHAPE ARMHOLE Cast off 4 sts at beg of next 2 rows. Dec 1 st at both ends of next and every alt row 11 times (106 sts). Cont in patt as set until row 132 is completed.

SHAPE SHOULDER AND NECK Cast off 10 sts at beg of next row and work to end. Cast off 10 sts at beg of next row, work 24 sts, and leave rem 62 sts on a st holder. Turn, dec 1 st at beg (neck edge) of next row, and work to end. Cast off 11 sts at beg of next row, work to last 2 sts, then p2tog. Work 1 row and cast off.

YARN
Rowan Cotton Glacé (cols A, B, C in colorway 2, D, E in colorway 1, F, G, H, I); Rowan Donegal Lambswool Tweed (cols C in colorway 1, E in colorway 2)

Key		Colorway 1	Colorway 2	Quantity	
☐	A	Terracotta 786	Parade 430	10 balls	x 50g
☒	B	Dijon 739	Kiwi 443	1 ball	x 50g
⊡	C	Eau-de-nil 458		2 hanks	x 25g
			Sweet Pea 781	1 ball	x 50g
◎	D	Blood Orange 445	Swimming Pool 438	1 ball	x 50g
⊟	E	Dusk 439		1 ball	x 50g
			Jewel 455	2 hanks	x 25g
▽	F	Delft 782	Carnival 432	1 ball	x 50g
☑	G	Lilac Wine 440	Air Force 442	1 ball	x 50g
△	H	Swimming Pool 438	Delft 782	1 ball	x 50g
⊞	I	Air Force 442	Provence 744	1 ball	x 50g

SWEATER CHART

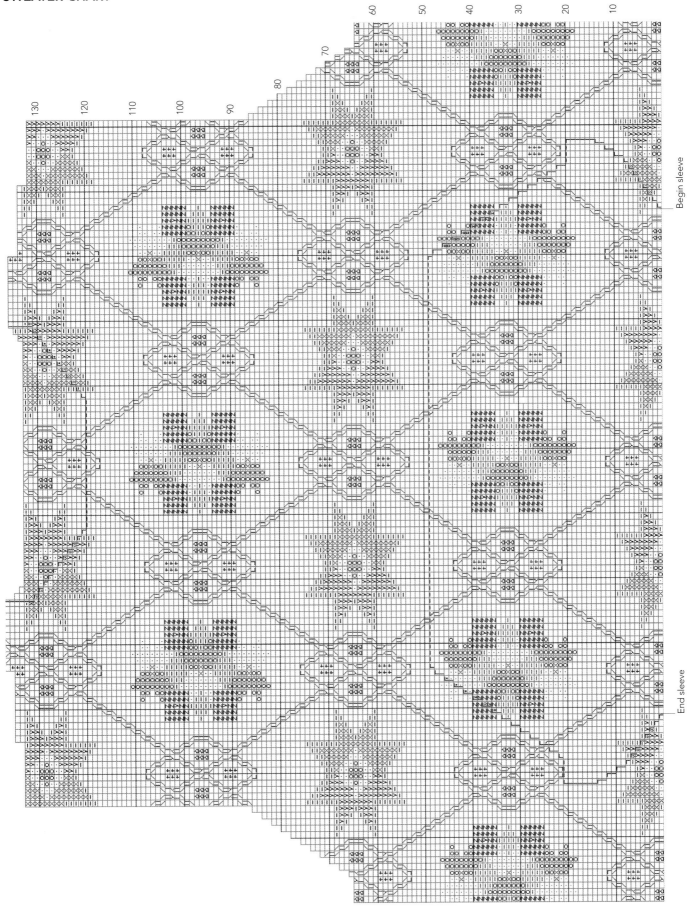

SWEATER STITCH KEY

⃞	rev st st in col A—purl on RS and knit on WS
✳	yarn forward and over needle to make a st
◢	k2tog
▲	p3tog
⋊⋋ ⟋⟍	right twist—k2tog and leave on needle, insert RH needle between sts just knitted tog and knit first st again, then sl both sts from LH needle
⋊⋋ ⟍	left twist—skip 1 st and knit the second st in back loop, then k2tog-b (skipped st and knit st) and sl both sts from needle tog

Rejoin yarn and cast off center 38 sts and work to end. Cast off 11 sts at beg of next row, work to last 2 sts, then k2tog. Dec 1 st at beg (neck edge) of next row and work to end. Cast off rem 11 sts.

FRONT

Work as for back until row 120 is completed.

SHAPE NECK Foll chart, work 43 sts, turn, and leave rem 63 sts on a st holder. Dec 1 st at neck edge on next and every foll row 11 times. Work 1 row. Cast off 10 sts at beg of next row. Work 1 row. Cast off 11 sts at beg of next row. Work 1 row. Cast off rem 11 sts. Rejoin yarn and cast off center 20 sts, then work to end. Dec 1 st at neck edge on next and every foll row 11 times. Work 2 rows. Cast off 10 sts at beg of next row. Work 1 row. Cast off 11 sts at beg of next row. Work 1 row. Cast off rem 11 sts.

SLEEVES

Using 3.75mm needles and col A, cast on 78 sts. Foll chart, work 1 row. Inc 1 st at both ends of next and every foll row 8 times (94 sts) and then every alt row 3 times (100 sts). Cont in patt as set until row 20 is completed.

SHAPE SLEEVE TOP Cast off 4 sts at beg of next 2 rows. Dec 1 st at both ends of next and every alt row 14 times. Cast off rem 64 sts purlwise on row 50.

LACY BORDER FOR FRONT AND BACK

Using 3.25mm needles and col A, cast on 22 sts. Foll back and front lacy border chart on the facing page, rep the 12 rows until work measures approx 42 in. and ends with a full patt rep. Leave on a st holder.

LACY BORDER FOR SLEEVES (MAKE 2)

Using 3.25mm needles and col A, cast on 10 sts. Foll sleeve lacy border chart on the facing page, rep the 12 rows until work measures approx 11½ in. and ends with a full patt rep. Leave on a st holder.

COLLAR

Using 3mm needles and col A, cast on 16 sts. Foll collar lacy border chart on the facing page, rep the 12 rows until work is approx same size as neck opening and ends with a full patt rep. Leave sts on a st holder.

FINISHING

Use a small, neat backstitch on edge of work for seams. Join shoulder seams, taking care that the cast-off edges do not show on RS and that a smooth slope results. Insert sleeves, spreading any extra fullness evenly over whole sleeve cap. Join side and sleeve seams in one line.
Using a small slipstitch, neatly attach straight edge of border to back and front from side seam to side seam, making sure that it fits snugly when stretched slightly.
Cast off the border when it fits perfectly. Attach sleeve borders similarly. Attach collar from center front to center front (as shirt collar), with RS of collar facing WS of neckline. Start at left center front, pin in place around neck, and finish at right center front, giving slight ease to collar so that it will fall without stretching on RS when slipstitched in place. Take care that the collar meets neatly at center front. Join side seams of borders using a neat slipstitch so they lie flat.

BACK AND FRONT LACY BORDER

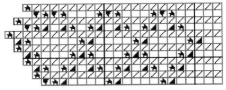

SLEEVE LACY BORDER

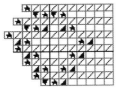

COLLAR LACY BORDER

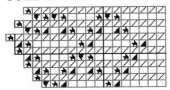

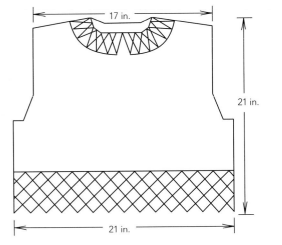

17 in.

21 in.

21 in.

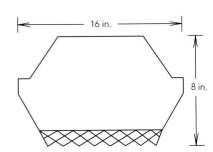

16 in.

8 in.

YARN

Rowan Magpie Aran (cols A, D, E, F, H); Rowan Chunky Cotton Chenille (cols B, C, G)

Key		Colorway 1	Colorway 2	Quantity	
⃫	A	Speedwell 508	Forest Green 362	2 hanks	x 100g
⃝	B	Forest Green 362	Speedwell 508	1 hank	x 100g
⃟	C	Claret 376	Comanche 503	1 hank	x 100g
⊞	D	Sienna 766	Aubergine 356	1 hank	x 100g
⊡	E	Ember 763	Sienna 766	1 hank	x 100g
✱	F	Comanche 503	Ember 763	4 hanks	x 100g
◣	G	Aubergine 356	Serge 378	1 hank	x 100g
△	H	Turq 308	Cork 309	1 hank	x 100g

PILLOW

NEEDLES
• 5mm (USA 8)
• 4.5mm (USA 7)

TENSION
18 sts and 26 rows = 4 in. over patt for front and different patt for back

MEASUREMENTS
22 in. by 23¾ in.

Baluch pillow in colorway 1 (left) and colorway 2

PILLOW STITCH KEY
☒   rev st st in col F—purl on RS and knit on WS

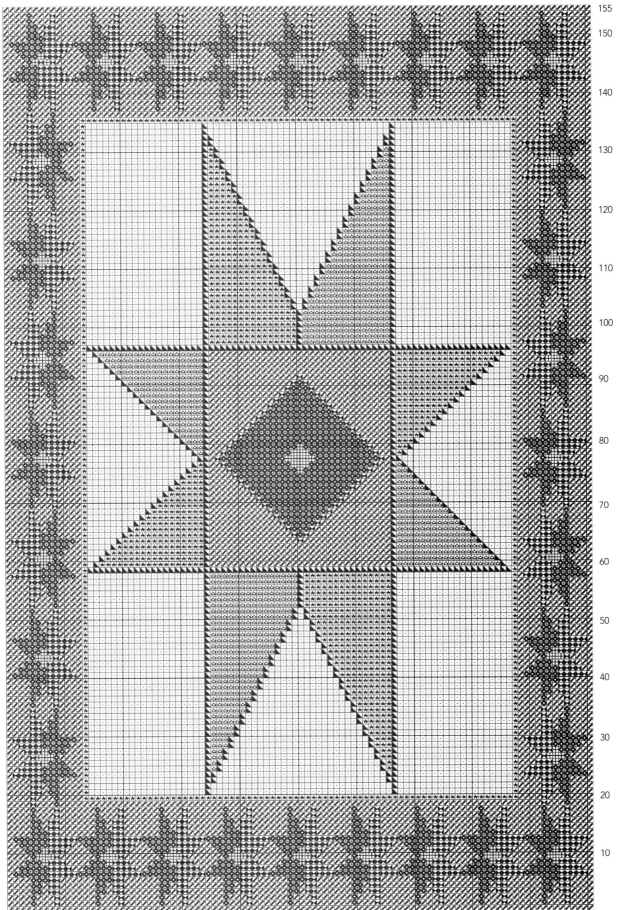

155
150
140
130
120
110
100
90
80
70
60
50
40
30
20
10

PILLOW CHART 2

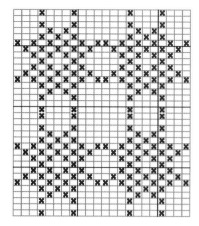

PILLOW CHART 3

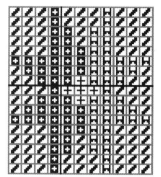

FRONT

Using 5mm needles and col A, cast on 101 sts. Foll chart 1 on p. 49, work the 155 rows and cast off.

BACK

Using 4.5mm needles and col F, cast on 101 sts and purl 1 row. Foll chart 2 above, work the 34 rows twice as follows:

ROW 1 Sl 1, work the 22 sts 4 times across row, work sts 1 to 11 inclusive, k1tbl.

ROW 2 Work as for row 1 but from left to right. After 68 rows have been worked, foll chart 2 for the next 17 rows, but insert the colored star from chart 3 above in center over sts 46 to 56 inclusive. (Back of pillow consists of rev st st stars with one colored star in the center.) Foll chart 2, work a further 68 rows. Purl 2 rows to form foldline, then work a further 3 in. in st st. Cast off loosely.

FINISHING

Use a small, neat backstitch on inside of pillow for all seams. Fold hem at top of back onto WS and slipstitch in place down side seams (not across cast-off edge). Seam the three other sides on inside so the top is open when turned RS out.

Baluch socks in colorway 2 (left) and colorway 1

SOCKS

NEEDLES

• Set of five double-pointed 4.5mm (USA 7)
• Set of five double-pointed 3.75mm (USA 5)
• Tapestry needle

TENSION

24 sts and 30 rows = 4 in. or 10cm over patt

MEASUREMENTS

To fit U.S. shoe sizes 5½ to 8½ (English sizes 4 to 7)

LEFT SOCK

Using 4.5mm needles and two-color cast-on method (see p. 7), cast on 1 st in col A, 1 st in col B, 1 st in col A, 2 sts in col B, 1 st in col A, 2 sts in col B. Working back and forth, work 3 rows in st st as follows:

YARN

Rowan Designer DK (cols A, B, C); Rowan Lightweight DK (col D)

Key		Colorway 1	Colorway 2	Quantity	
☐	A	Teal Green 661	Rust 663	1 ball	x 50g
⊙	B	Navy 671	Navy 671	2 balls	x 50g
☑	C	Rust 663	Teal Green 661	1 ball	x 50g
⊞	D	Red 46	Red 46	1 hank	x 25g

ROW 1 K1 col B, k3 col A, k1 col B, k3 col A.

ROW 2 P1 col A, p1 col B, p1 col A, p2 col B, p1 col A, p2 col B.

ROW 3 K5 col B, k3 col A.
Beg knitting in the round, as there will be a needle at each end of the strip. Rotate the work to the side edge of the knitted strip. With the third needle, pick up and knit 2 sts in col A across this edge, one st each in the middle of the st at the end of every other row. Rotate and work k3 col A, k5 col B across the initial cast-on

SOCKS STITCH KEY

⊡ purl in col A

SOCKS CHART 1

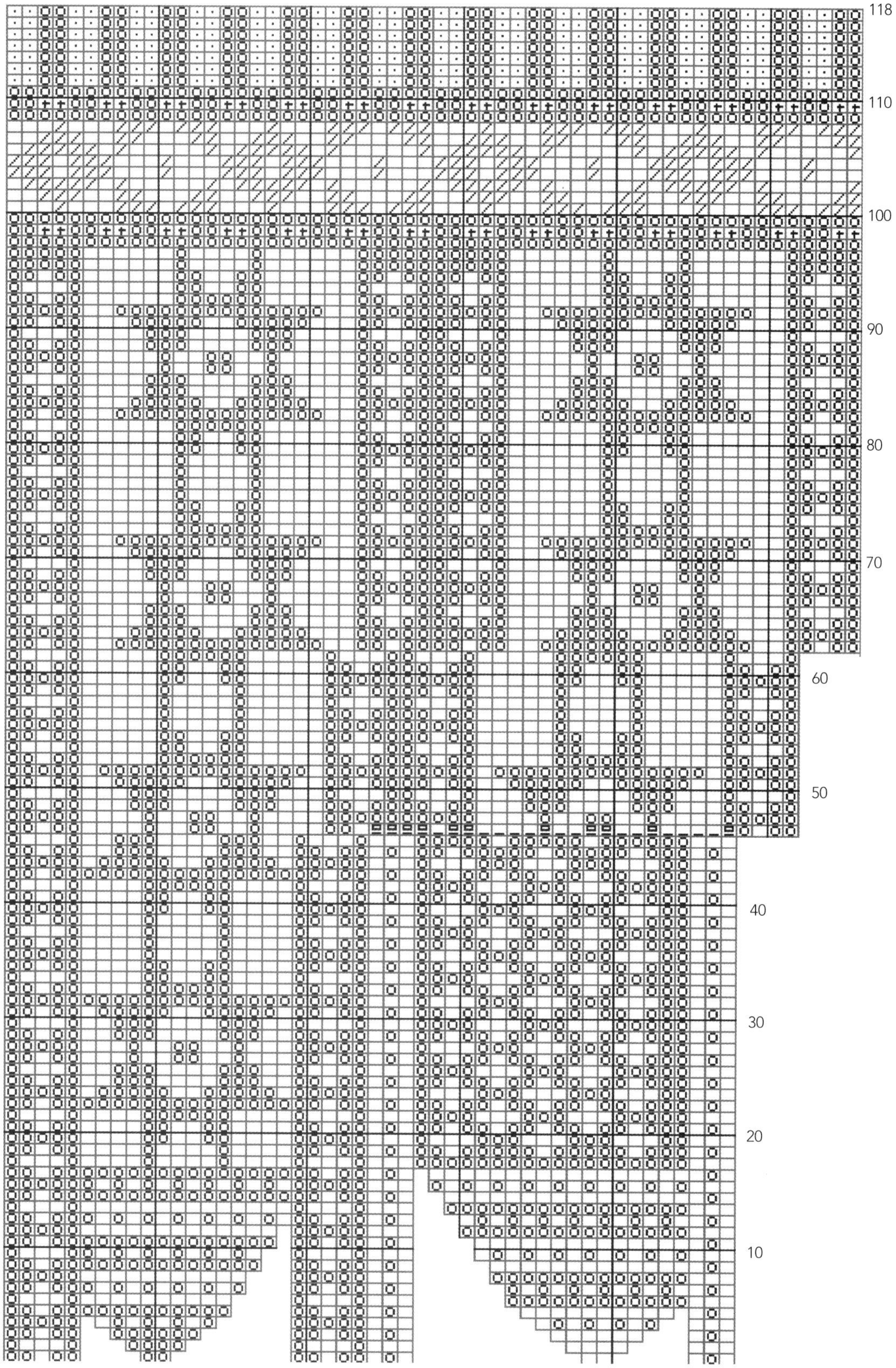

sts. Rotate and rep the pick up and knit 2 sts in col B along the final edge (20 sts).

The work is now in a rectangle. Reposition the sts so that each rnd starts with the last 3 sts of the cast-on row so that sts are in position for first rnd of chart 1 on the facing page.

TOE SHAPING **Note:** As you are working in the round in st st, all rows are knit rows and chart is read from right to left on every rnd.

Foll chart 1, work the 118 rnds as follows:

RND 1 Work 3 sts, make 1 st, work 2 sts, make 1 st, work 8 sts, make 1 st, work 2 sts, make 1 st, work 5 sts.

RND 2 Work 3 sts, make 1 st, work 4 sts, make 1 st, work 8 sts, make 1 st, work 4 sts, make 1 st, work 5 sts.

Cont shaping as set from chart 1, inc 4 times in each rnd to rnd 13 on inside of edging sts, then twice in each rnd to rnd 18. Cont until rnd 46 is completed, then leave the 24 sts indicated on chart 1 on a st holder.

RND 47 Cast on 26 sts using backward loop method in the col patt of rnd 47 on chart 1. Cont around in patt, making 1 st between sts 31 and 32 and between sts 45 and 46 (just inside the braid patt edging) (52 sts). Cont until rnd 61 is completed.

RND 62 Make 1 st between sts 5 and 6, 21 and 22, 31 and 32, 45 and 46 (56 sts). Cont until rnd 111 is completed. Change to 3.75mm needles and work 7 rnds in k2, p2 striped rib. Cast off loosely in col B.

HEEL To insert heel, pick up 24 sts from st holder and 26 sts from the backward loop cast-on sts. The back heel sts will be running in the other direction compared to the sts of the back leg, but the color alignment of the patt should be true. Foll chart 2 at right, work heel, dec 2 sts on rnd 1 by knitting tog sts 30 and 31, 44 and 45, and then as indicated on chart.

Note: Sole and instep shapings are different.

RND 9 K3, sl 1, k1, psso, k14, k2tog, k8, sl 1, k1, psso, k10, k2tog, k5. Cont dec as set on inside of edging sts.

To close the heel, rearrange the sts and graft the two side panels together by placing the first 3 and last 5 sts on one needle and holding at back. Place the middle 8 sts on another needle and hold at front.

Thread tapestry needle with col B and use Kitchener st (see p. 9) over the 8 double sts. When all sts are used up, pull yarn through to WS and fasten off securely.

RIGHT SOCK

Work as for left sock cast on for 4 rows, then position the sts to keep chart 3 correct. Foll chart 3 for right toe below, work the 18 rnds. Cont as for left sock from rnd 19 on chart 1, but rev the sole and instep patts, working the heel sts on the left of chart at top of sole sts, as set by patt on rnd 18.

SOCKS CHART 2

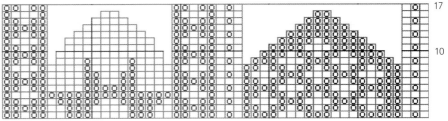

SOCKS CHART 3

ALBION

SWEATER

THROW

HAT

PILLOW

Samplers are a wonderful guide to the popular stitches and patterns of their time. Queens and kings, houses and hearts, flowers and trees, birds and bees, butterflies, banners, bowls of fruit, angels, and more— they all play their parts in the unfolding drama of the sampler through the centuries. The first datable English sampler was worked by Jane Bostocke in Elizabeth I's reign in 1598. I prefer, though, the pieces made in the late 18th and early 19th centuries, when needlework was at its most naive.

The Yorkshire sampler pictured above was embroidered in 1817 by 15-year-old Ruth Jessop. It is worked in cross-stitch with silk thread on coarse linen canvas. In the Albion sweater, I have followed the same biblical tradition of depicting life's cycle in an ascending order, starting with the physical world of the plants and animals and working up to the celestial realm of god, angels, and spirits. Hearts have always been one of my favorite

motifs: I have developed the Jacobean ladies into majestic Elizabethan queens, using the heart motif for their bodices. In true sampler tradition, I could not resist adding the banner *Amor vincit omnia,* which means "love conquers all." You could substitute your own words if you wish. As the underwater world is not represented in the knitting, I added the hand-carved fish button on the collar to complete the design. This sweater is not for the novice knitter but is well within the capabilities of someone who enjoys intarsia.

The theme is continued with the Albion throw and pillow: the throw is an interesting introduction to intarsia knitting, and the pillow is arguably the easiest piece of intarsia you will ever knit. It seems appropriate that with all the hearts in this chapter the Albion hat should be finished with a red rose. If you're not confident with the intarsia on the band, simply omit it or stripe the band in the two colors from the rose.

Photo courtesy of The Castle Museum, York

Detail of Albion sweater in colorway 1

Previous page: Albion throw, sweater, and hat in colorway 2, and sweater and hat in colorway 1

SWEATER

NEEDLES

- 2.75mm (USA 2)
- 3.25mm (USA 3)
- Set of four 2.75mm (USA 2) double-pointed needles

BUTTON

One fish-shaped 30mm by 7mm

TENSION

28 sts and 36 rows = 4 in. or 10cm over intarsia patt

SIZE

One size to fit 34-in. to 40-in. bust
See diagram on p. 61 for finished knitted measurements.

YARN

Rowan 4-ply Botany (cols A, B, C, D, E, F in colorway 1, G, K, L in colorway 2, N); Rowan Donegal Lambswool Tweed (cols H, J); Rowan Kid Silk (cols F in colorway 2, I, L in colorway 1, M)

Key		Colorway 1	Colorway 2	Quantity	
☐	A	Iris 556	Jet 546	10 balls	x 50g
☒	B	Camouflage 562	Pine 553	1 ball	x 50g
⊙	C	Nettle 551	Nettle 551	1 ball	x 50g
⊘	D	Conker 555	Conker 555	1 ball	x 50g
⊞	E	Plum 547	Plum 547	1 ball	x 50g
☒	F	Redwood 549		1 ball	x 50g
			Crushed Berry 993	2 balls	x 25g
⊻	G	Navy 563	Iris 556	1 ball	x 50g
⊟	H	Eau-de-nil 458	Eau-de-nil 458	2 hanks	x 25g
△	I	Old Gold 989	Old Gold 989	2 balls	x 25g
ⓢ	J	Acid 447	Acid 447	2 hanks	x 25g
✳	K	Sorrel 550	Sorrel 550	1 ball	x 50g
Ⓜ	L	Crushed Berry 993		1 ball	x 25g
			Redwood 549	1 ball	x 50g
◹	M	Opal 976	Opal 976	1 ball	x 25g
◆	N	Prince 557	Prince 557	1 ball	x 50g

BACK

Using 2.75mm needles and col A, cast on 162 sts. Foll chart 1 on pp. 58-59, work the first 30 rows. Change to 3.25mm needles and cont to work from chart until row 164 is completed.

SHAPE ARMHOLE   Dec 1 st at both ends of next and every alt row 14 times in all, until there are 134 sts. Cont foll chart until row 252 is completed.

SHAPE SHOULDER AND NECKLINE   Cast off 15 sts at beg of next row, work to end. Cast off 15 sts at beg of next row, work 34 sts, then leave rest of sts on a st holder. Turn. Dec 1 st at beg of next row, work to end. Cast off 16 sts at beg of next row, work to last 2 sts, p2tog. Work 1 row, then cast off the rem 16 sts.
Work other side of neck to match. Leave the center 36 sts on a st holder and rejoin yarn to the rem 34 sts. Work 1 row. Cast off 16 sts at beg of next row, work to last 2 sts, k2tog. Dec 1 st at beg of next row, work to end. Cast off the rem 16 sts.

FRONT

Work as for back until row 201 is completed.

SHAPE NECKLINE   Work 65 sts, p2tog, turn, and place the rem 67 sts on a st holder. Cont to work from chart, dec 1 st at neck edge every alt row until there are 56 sts and then at neck edge every third row until there are 47 sts. Cont to work from chart until row 253 is completed.

SHAPE SHOULDER   Cast off 15 sts at beg of next row, work to end. Work 1 row. Cast off 16 sts at beg of next row, work to end. Work 1 row. Cast off the rem 16 sts. Rejoin yarn at center front and dec 1 st at beg of next and every alt row 11 times (56 sts), and then at neck edge every third row 9 times until there are 47 sts. Cont to work from chart until row 252 is completed.

SHAPE SHOULDER   Cast off 15 sts at beg of next row, work to end. Work 1 row. Cast off 16 sts at beg of next row, work to end. Work 1 row. Cast off the rem 16 sts.

SLEEVES

Using 2.75mm needles and col A, cast on 70 sts. Foll chart 2 on pp. 60-61, work the first 30 rows. Change to 3.25mm needles and cont foll chart, inc 1 st at both ends of next and every fourth row until there are 90 sts and then every fifth row until there are 134 sts. Cont foll chart until row 188 is completed, then cast off.

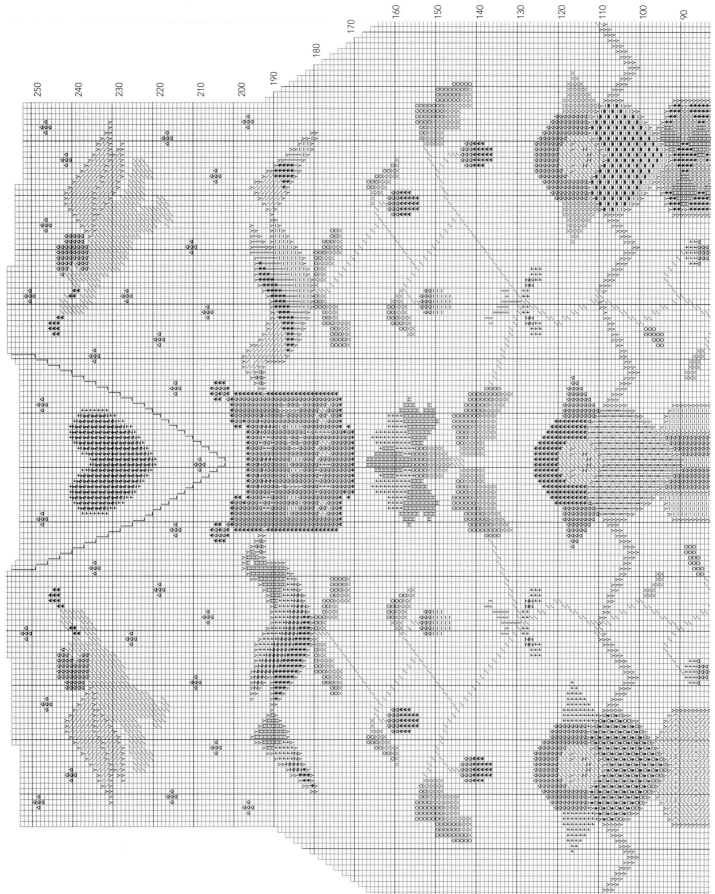

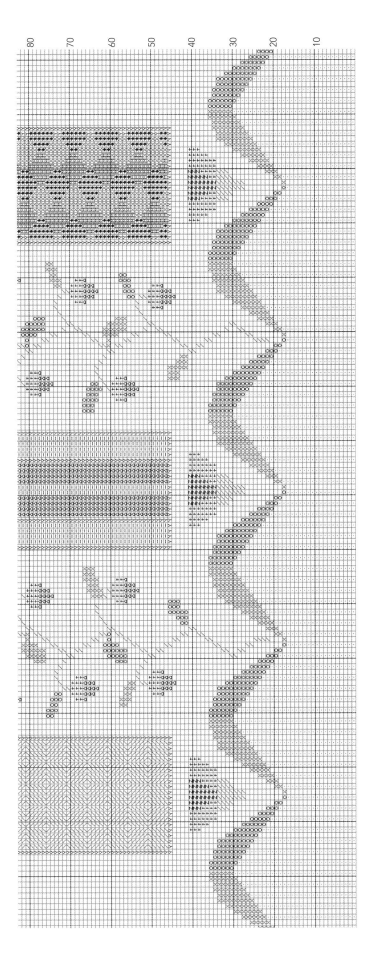

SWEATER STITCH KEY

⊡	rev st st in col A—purl on RS and knit on WS
⦿	rev st st in col C
⊠	rev st st in col F
⊟	rev st st in col H
⧈	rev st st in col K

SWEATER CHART 2: SLEEVE

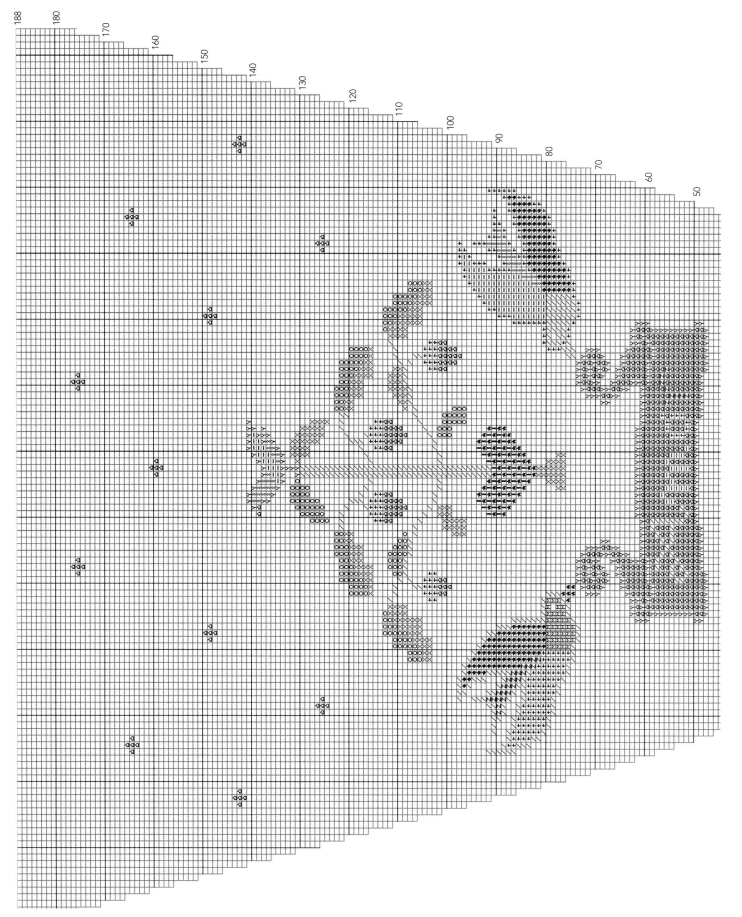

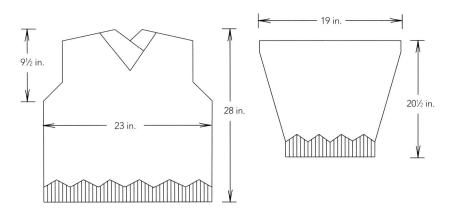

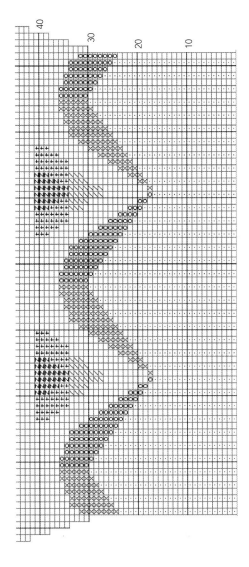

COLLAR

Join shoulder seams using a small, neat back-stitch on the edge of work, but make sure that the cast-off edge does not show on the RS. Using four double-pointed 2.75mm needles and col A, with RS facing and starting at right center front, pick up and knit 48 sts up sloping edge of right front neck; 8 sts up straight edge to shoulder; 4 sts down right back neck edge; 36 sts from st holder at center back; 4 sts up left back neck edge; 8 sts down straight edge of left neck edge; and 48 sts down sloping neck edge to center front (156 sts).

Working in rows and not in the round, work collar in moss st as follows:

ROW 1 *K1, p1, rep from * to end.

ROW 2 *P1, k1, rep from * to end.
Rep these 2 rows until collar measures 2¼ in. and ends on a RS row.

WORK BUTTONHOLE Starting at right front edge, work 4 sts, turn, work a further 4 rows, then leave these sts on a st holder. Rejoin yarn and work across rem sts for 5 rows, then on sixth row work across all sts. Work a further 2 rows and cast off.

FINISHING

Use a small, neat backstitch on edge of work for all seams except ribs, where an invisible edge-to-edge stitch should be used so the ribs lie flat. Insert sleeves, placing the straight edge of the sleeves along the armhole edge of the sweater. Join side and sleeve seams in one line. Sew on button opposite buttonhole.

THROW

NEEDLES
• Circular 3.75mm (USA 5)
• Circular 3.25mm (USA 3)

TENSION
26 sts and 33 rows = 4 in. or 10cm over patt

MEASUREMENTS
68 in. by 49 in.

YARN
Rowan Lightweight DK

Key		Color	Quantity	
□	A*	Cinnamon 136	10 hanks	x 25g
□	B**	Teal 91	14 hanks	x 25g
·	C	Petrol 54	26 hanks	x 25g
O	D	Olive 407	4 hanks	x 25g
/	E	Brick 45	6 hanks	x 25g
\	F	Purple 149	6 hanks	x 25g
+	G	Celadon 100	4 hanks	x 25g
V	H	Rust 27	8 hanks	x 25g
S	I	Slate 88	4 hanks	x 25g

* Use col A for background labeled A on throw chart 1
** Use col B for background labeled B on throw chart 1

KNITTING THE THROW
Note: Patt is worked back and forth, *not* in the round.

Using a 3.75mm needle, cast on 289 sts as follows: 49 sts in col A, 11 sts in col C, 49 sts in col B, 11 sts in col C, 49 sts in col A, 11 sts in col C, 49 sts in col B, 11 sts in col C, 49 sts in col A (289 sts).

Foll chart 1 on p. 64 and reading RS rows from right to left and WS rows from left to right, rep the 156 rows three times as follows:

ROW 1   Work 120 sts of chart twice, then work the first 49 sts (289 sts).

ROW 2   Work the last 49 sts, then work the full 120 sts twice (289 sts).

Work as set keeping patt correct until 3 rep have been worked (row 468). Work a further 65 rows of patt and cast off.

Note: Each colored section should be cast off in the same color as on cast-on edge.

BORDER
Using 3.25mm needles and col C, with RS facing, pick up and knit 448 sts along the length of throw. Purl 1 row. Foll chart 2 on p. 64, work the 15 rows, inc 1 st at both ends of every row. Work patt as follows:

ROW 1   Work the last 8 sts, work the 36 sts 12 times, work the first 8 sts (448 sts).

ROW 2   Work the last 8 sts, work the 36 sts 12 times, work the first 8 sts.

THROW STITCH KEY

X	rev st st in col C—purl on RS and knit on WS
◪	rev st st in col E
◩	rev st st in col F
▣	rev st st in col G
▼	rev st st in col H
▮	rev st st in col I

Albion throw

THROW CHART 1

THROW CHART 2

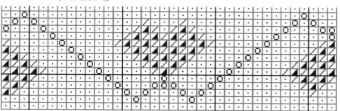

Note: As you inc, incorporate 1 st more of the patt at both ends until row 15. On row 15, work the last 22 sts, work the 36 sts 12 times, work the first 22 sts.

Using col C to end, knit 1 row to form foldline for hem. Work 15 rows in st st, dec 1 st at both ends of every row. Cast off. Work similarly along other long side of throw.

Using 3.25mm needles and col C, with RS facing, pick up and knit 312 sts along the width of throw. Purl 1 row. Foll chart 2 on the facing page, work the 15 rows, inc 1 st at both ends of every row. Work patt as follows:

ROW 1 Work the last 12 sts, work the 36 sts 8 times, work the first 12 sts (312 sts). Incorporate the extra sts into patt as you inc until row 15. On row 15, work the last 26 sts, work the 36 sts 8 times, work the first 26 sts. Using col C to end, knit 1 row to form foldline for hem. Work 15 rows in st st, dec 1 st at both ends of every row. Cast off. Work similarly along other short side of throw.

FINISHING

Join diagonal edges of border with an invisible slipstitch, matching patt and rows. Fold the borders to inside and stitch in place using an invisible slipstitch. As the throw is not reversible, make sure that all ends are worked in securely and neatly so the WS of throw looks as attractive as possible. Swiss darn "I love my home" in first square on right in cols indicated on chart 3 below.

THROW CHART 3

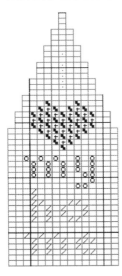

Albion hat in colorway 1

HAT

NEEDLES
- Set of four 3mm (USA 2)
- Set of four 3.75mm (USA 5)

TENSION
24 sts and 30 rows = 4 in. or 10cm over st st for crown

MEASUREMENTS
22-in. circumference

YARN
Rowan Lightweight DK

Key		Colorway 1	Colorway 2	Quantity	
☐	A	Black 62	Navy 151	5 hanks	x 25g
⧄	B	Lovat Green 655	Teal Green 91	1 hank	x 25g
☒	C	Russet 132	Rust 77	1 hank	x 25g
⊙	D	Claret 46	Old Gold 9	1 hank	x 25g

HAT STITCH KEY

ꟸ   rev st st in col C—purl on RS, knit on WS

Ⅴ   rev st st in col A

Ⅿ   from behind, insert needle under the running thread (the strand running from the base of the st just worked to the base of the next st) and lift this thread onto the LH needle, then knit 1 st into the back of it

d   single dec—lift the last worked st back onto the LH needle and lift the next unworked st over it and off the needle, then return this to the RH needle

BAND
Using 3mm needles and col A, cast on 140 sts, then divide evenly over three needles and commence working with the fourth. Work 13 rnds in k1, p1 rib, then purl 1 row to form fold for hem. Foll chart 1 below, work the 13 rnds in st st, working the 28 sts 5 times around (all rows are read from right to left as you are working in the rnd).

CROWN
Change to 3.75mm needles and cont in col A. Foll chart 2 below, work the 78 rnds, working the 14 sts 10 times around and inc 1 st on first and every sixth rnd 5 times in all (240 sts). Then dec 1 st on rnd 34 and every fourth rnd 11 times in all (20 sts), working dec on purl row on rnds 42 and 70.

NEXT ROW   K2tog on every st (10 sts). Break yarn, leaving a 10-in. tail. Thread through all sts and fasten off securely on WS.

FINISHING
Turn facing (k1, p1 rib) to WS and sew neatly in place along inside. From a piece of felt, cut out two leaves and a long, narrow piece for the rose. To create the rose shape, twist the narrow piece tightly and wind it around itself. Stitch onto band using neat, invisible sts.

HAT CHART 1

HAT CHART 2

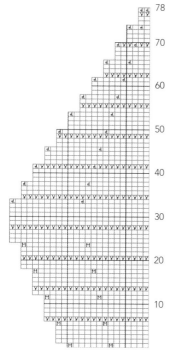

PILLOW

NEEDLES

• 4.5mm (USA 7)

• 4.5mm crochet hook

TENSION

21 sts and 27 rows = 4 in. or 10cm over st st

Note: All yarn is used doubled

MEASUREMENTS

16 in. by 16 in.

Albion pillow in colorway 1 (left)
and colorway 2

YARN

Rowan Donegal Lambswool Tweed (cols A, B, E, F in colorway 2, H, L);
Rowan Fine Cotton Chenille (cols D, G in colorway 2, J, K in colorway 1);
Rowan 4-ply Botany (cols C, F in colorway 1, G in colorway 1, I, K in colorway 2)

Key		Colorway 1	Colorway 2	Quantity	
□	A	1 strand Teal 456	1 strand Pine 553	3 hanks	x 25g
	B	1 strand Juniper 482	1 strand Bay 485	2 hanks	x 25g
⊘	C	1 strand Redwood 549	1 strand Redwood 549	1 ball	x 50g
	D	1 strand Ruby 407	1 strand Ruby 407	1 ball	x 50g
⊡	E	1 strand Cinnamon 479	1 strand Woad 460	3 hanks	x 25g
	F	1 strand Conker 555		2 balls	x 50g
			1 strand Teal 456	2 hanks	x 25g
⊟	G	1 strand Pine 553	1 strand Privet 410	1 ball	x 50g
	H	1 strand Bay 485	1 strand Bark 475	1 hank	x 25g
⊙	I	1 strand Redwood 549	1 strand Redwood 549		
	J	1 strand Plum 409	1 strand Plum 409	1 ball	x 50g
⊿	K	1 strand Privet 410		1 ball	x 50g
			1 strand Conker 555	1 ball	x 50g
	L	1 strand Juniper 482	1 strand Cinnamon 479		

PILLOW CHART 1

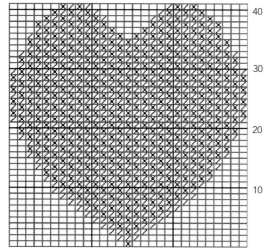

PIECE 1

Note: Use two strands of yarn throughout the pillow.

Using 4.5mm needles and cols A and B, cast on 83 sts. Foll chart 1 at left, work the 41 rows as follows:

ROW 1 Work 27 sts in st st, work the 29 sts of chart 1, work 27 sts in st st.
Work 29 rows as set above, work a further 33 rows in cols A and B in st st, then cast off (108 rows).

PIECE 2

Using 4.5mm needles and cols E and F, cast on 83 sts and work 34 rows in st st. Foll chart 2 on the facing page, work the 39 rows as follows:

ROW 1 Work 23 sts in st st, work the 37 sts of chart 2, work 23 sts in st st.
Work 39 rows as set above, then work a further 35 rows in cols E and F in st st (108 rows). Purl 2 rows to mark hem. Work a further 3 in. in st st in cols E and F and cast off loosely.

FINISHING

Turn down hem onto inside and slipstitch in place down side seams (not across cast-off edge).
Using a 4.5mm crochet hook and 2 strands of col D, work 2 rows of dc (see p. 9) around the four sides of pillow, placing wrong sides together with RS on outside. Dc across the top of piece 1, then crochet along the other three edges of pieces 1 and 2, working through both pieces together. Work 1 more row, then fasten off neatly and securely.

PILLOW CHART 2

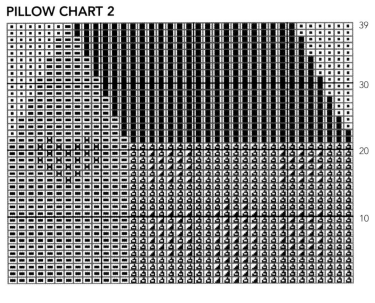

PILLOW STITCH KEY

☒   rev st st in cols C and D—purl on RS, knit on WS

◨   rev st st in cols G and H

◼   rev st st in cols C and J

◪   rev st st in cols K and B (colorway 1); K and L (colorway 2)

LISDOONVARNA

JACKET

THROW

PILLOW

SOCKS

Named after the annual matchmaking festival in County Clare, the Lisdoonvarna collection is inspired by the arans and cables of the West of Ireland, such as the one shown above. Just as the festival is a celebration of coupling, the following pages are a celebration of the beauty of knitted stitchery and myriad sculptured effects that can be achieved with one color. To knit an aran you need know only two stitches, knit and purl, but the combinations of these give rise to an infinite palette of intricate stitchery with which to paint these wonderful textured pictures.

The subject of past speculation about its religious symbolism, aran stitchwork also has a down-to-earth explanation: it traps air to provide the fisherfolk with excellent insulation and protection against the wild Atlantic weather. One can see, though, a connection between the islanders' environment and their stitchwork: between a harsh landscape of stony fields, drystone walls,

restless seas, and rocky cliffs and the rugged sculpture of knots, cables, plaits, and trellises that typify aran knitting.

In the Lisdoonvarna jacket, throw, pillow, and socks, there is a selection of stitches that you can mix or match, depending on your mood or expertise. The throw is the most demanding knit, involving the use of all five stitch patterns, but it will become a lifelong heirloom for you to cherish. If you are not confident with so many different patterns in one piece, it would also look stunning knitted in the pillow pattern. Rather than the familiar off-white bawneen, I have made the jacket in the traditional indigo blue. The hand-carved cartwheel bone buttons reflect the pattern at the hem and cuffs. This is certainly an interesting knit for anyone who enjoys aran knitting. I recommend the pillow and socks for those who have not yet tried aran knitting but want to get started. I can assure you that by the end of this chapter you will be hooked.

Lisdoonvarna jacket and Hausa pillow

Previous page: Lisdoonvarna jacket

JACKET

NEEDLES

- 3.25mm (USA 3)
- 3.75mm (USA 5)
- 4.5mm (USA 7)
- Cable needle

BUTTONS

Five 20mm

TENSION

24 sts and 30 rows = 4 in. or 10cm over patt (before shrinkage)

SIZE

One size to fit 34-in. to 40-in. bust
See diagram on p. 77 for finished knitted measurements.

WELT PATTERN

Row 1   Knit.

Row 2   Knit.

Row 3   K1, *yo, (k1b, p3) 5 times, k1b, yo, k1, rep from *.

Row 4   P3, *(k3, p1) 4 times, k3, p5, rep from *, end last rep p3.

YARN

Rowan Cotton Denim

Color	Quantity	
Nashville 225	20 balls	x 50g

Row 5   K1, *yo k1b, yo, (k1b, p3) 5 times, (k1b, yo) twice, k1, rep from *.

Row 6   P5, *(k3, p1) 4 times, k3, p9, rep from *, end last rep p5.

Row 7   K1, *yo, k1b, yo, ssk, yo, (k1b, p2tog, p1) 5 times, k1b, yo, k2tog, yo, k1b, yo, k1, rep from *.

Row 8   P7, *(k2, p1) 4 times, k2, p13, rep from *, end last rep p7.

Row 9   K1, *k1b, (yo, ssk) twice, yo, (k1b, p2) 5 times, k1b, yo, (k2tog, yo) twice, k1b, k1, rep from *.

Row 10   P8, *(k2, p1) 4 times, k2, p15, rep from *, end last rep p8.

Row 11   K2, *(yo, k2tog) twice, yo, k1b, yo, (k1b, p2tog) 5 times, (k1b, yo) twice, (ssk, yo) twice, k3, rep from *, end last rep k2.

Row 12   P10, *(k1, p1) 4 times, k1, p19, rep from *, end last rep p10.

Row 13   Ssk, *(yo, k2tog) 3 times, k1b, yo, (k1b, p1) 5 times, k1b, yo, k1b, (ssk, yo) 3 times, sl 2-k1-p2sso, rep from *, end last rep k2tog instead of sl 2-k1-p2sso.

Row 14   Rep row 12.

Row 15   K1, *(k2tog, yo) twice, k2tog, k1, k1b, yo, (ssk) twice, sl 1-k2-psso, (k2tog) twice, yo, k1b, k1, ssk, (yo, ssk) twice, k1, rep from *.

Row 16   Cluster (sl the given number of sts with yarn in back, pass yarn to front, sl the same number of sts back to LH needle, pass yarn back to back, sl the same sts again with yarn in back) 2, *p7, cluster 5, p7, cluster 3, rep from *, end last rep cluster 2 instead of cluster 3.

Row 17   Purl.

BACK

Using 3.75mm needles, cast on 133 sts and work first 17 rows in welt patt.

ROW 18 *P1, k1, M1, k1, p1, k4, p1, k3, rep from * to last st, p1 (144 sts).

ROW 19 K1, *p3, k1, p4, k1, p3, k1, rep from * to last 4 sts, p3, k1.

ROW 20 *P1, k3, p1, k4, p1, k3, rep from * to last st, p1.

ROW 21 Rep row 19.
Change to 4.5mm needles. Foll chart 1 on pp. 74-75, work 156 rows starting at left side on WS row. Work shaping for neck on chart row 153, leaving 30 sts at center back on spare needle. Cast off firmly on row 157.

FRONTS

Using 3.75mm needles, cast on 67 sts and work 17 rows in welt patt.

ROW 18 K3, *p1, k3, rep from *.

ROW 19 P3, *k1, p3, rep from *.

ROW 20 Rep row 18.

ROW 21 Rep row 19 to last st, inc 1 purlwise (68 sts).
Change to 4.5mm needles. Foll chart 2 on p. 76, work the 156 rows, starting on WS row. Work respective shapings for neck from chart row 79 by dec 1 st where indicated. Cast off firmly on row 157.

SLEEVES

Using 3.75mm needles, cast on 45 sts and work 17 rows in welt patt.

ROW 18 K2, *p1, k1, M1, k2, rep from * to last 3 sts, p1, k2 (55 sts).

ROW 19 P2, *k1, p2, M1, p2, k1, p4, rep from * to last 3 sts, k1, p2.

ROW 20 K2, *p1, k4, p1, k5, rep from * to last 3 sts, p1, k2.

ROW 21 P2, *k1, p5, k1, p4, rep from * to last 3 sts, k1, p2 (60 sts).
Change to 4.5mm needles. Foll chart 3 on p. 77, work the 108 rows, inc as indicated until there are 114 sts. Cast off firmly on row 109.

JACKET STITCH KEY

Note: Charts start on purl row (WS), reading from left to right. Read even-numbered rows from right to left.

□	st st—knit on RS and purl on WS
·	rev st st—knit on WS and purl on RS
⊘	on purl rows, p2tog
∕	on knit rows, k2tog
O	yarn over
X	no st
V	inc 1—(k1, k1 in back loop) in one st
\	on purl rows, p2tog-b—purl 1 st, return it to LH needle, then with point of RH needle pass next st over it and off needle, then sl the st back to RH needle
\	on knit rows, ssk—sl the first and second sts one at a time as if to knit, then insert point of LH needle into fronts of these 2 sts and knit them together
⅍	3 over 1 cross—sl 3 sts to cn and hold at front, p1, then k3 from cn
⅍	3 over 1 cross—sl 1 st to cn and hold at back, k3, then p1 from cn
⋊⋉	(A) 2 over 2 cross—sl 2 sts to cn and hold at front, k2, then k2 from cn
⋊⋉	(B) 2 over 2 cross—sl 2 sts to cn and hold at back, k2, then k2 from cn
⋊⋉	3 over 3 cross—sl 3 sts to cn and hold at front, k3, then k3 from cn
⋊⋉	3 over 3 cross—sl 3 sts to cn and hold at back, k3, then k3 from cn
⋊⋉⋊⋉	same as A and B above, worked over 8 sts

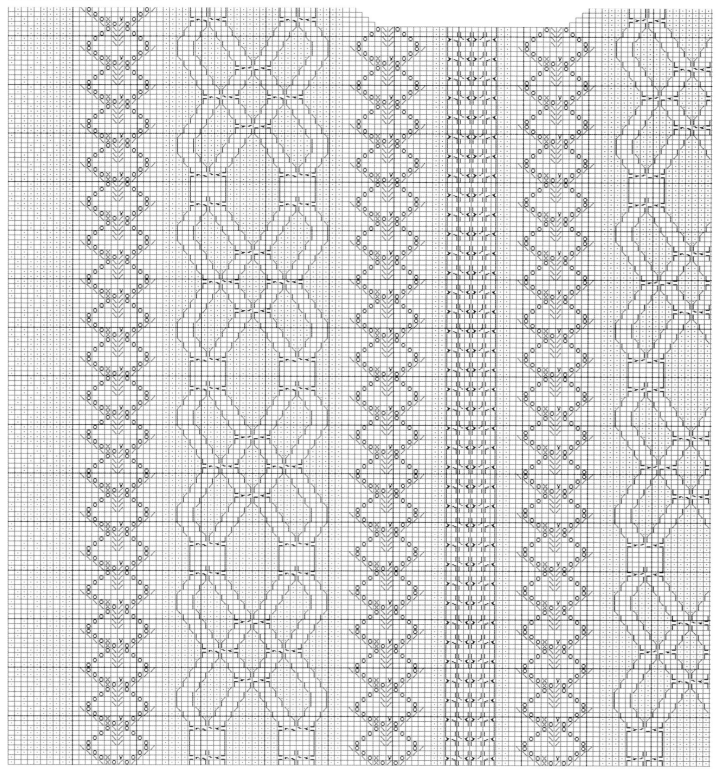

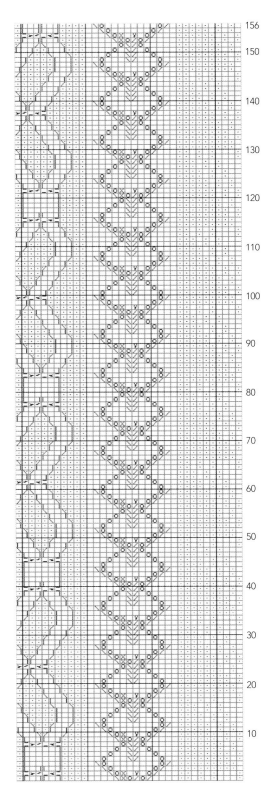

BUTTON BAND

Using 3.25mm needles, cast on 7 sts. Working in moss st (k1, *p1, k1, rep from * to end for every row), work band to fit left front. The band should start at top of welt patt and finish where neckline shaping begins. It should fit snugly when stretched slightly. Sew the band onto the front as you knit using an edge-to-edge slipstitch, and cast off when it fits perfectly.

BUTTONHOLE BAND

Mark position of 5 buttons on button band, the first ¾ in. from bottom, the fifth ½ in. from top, and the rem 3 spaced evenly between. Work band as for button band, working buttonholes as marked when you come to them as follows: Work 2 sts, cast off 3 sts, work 2 sts. Cast on these sts when you come to them on next row, knitting into backs on foll row.

COLLAR

Join shoulder seams using a small, neat backstitch on very edge of work. Using 3.25mm needles and starting in center of right front band (3 sts in from side edge) with RS facing, pick up and knit 58 sts to shoulder seam; 3 sts down back neck edge; 30 sts from st holder at center back; 3 sts up neck edge to shoulder; and 58 sts down left front, ending on center st of top of button band (152 sts).
Work in moss st as follows:

ROW 1   *K1, p1, rep from *.

ROW 2   *P1, k1, rep from *.
Rep these 2 rows until work measures 2½ in., then cast off loosely.

JACKET CHART 2: FRONTS

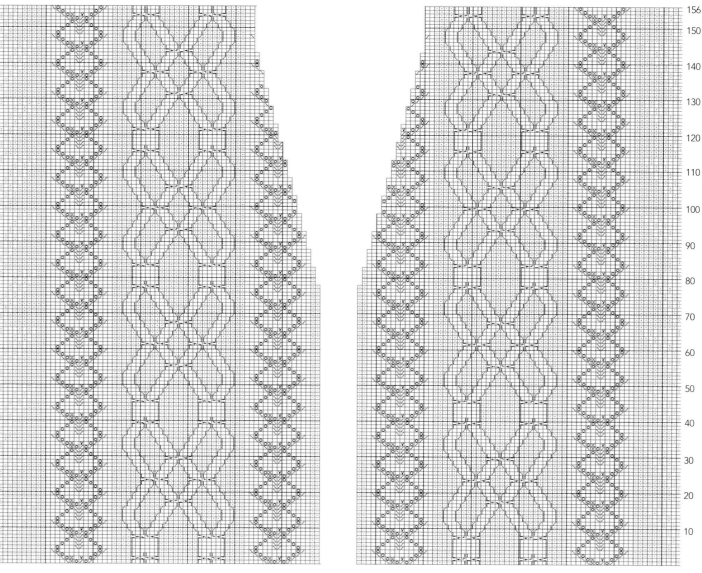

FINISHING

Before sewing together, wash all pieces in a washing machine at 140° to 160°F so shrinkage can take place. Wind some yarn that will be used for sewing the garment into a hank and wash along with the pieces. The pieces can be tumble dried on a moderate setting.

Turn down the collar and sew a tiny, invisible stitch around outside edge, ¼ in. from seam. Use a small, neat backstitch on very edge of

work for all seams. Find center of sleeve and mark. Place marker at shoulder seam and pin rest of sleeve in place and sew. Join side and sleeve seams in one line from top of welt to top of welt. Join welts using an invisible slipstitch so they lie completely flat. Attach 5 buttons to button band directly opposite buttonholes, aligning the patts on each side.

JACKET CHART 3: SLEEVE

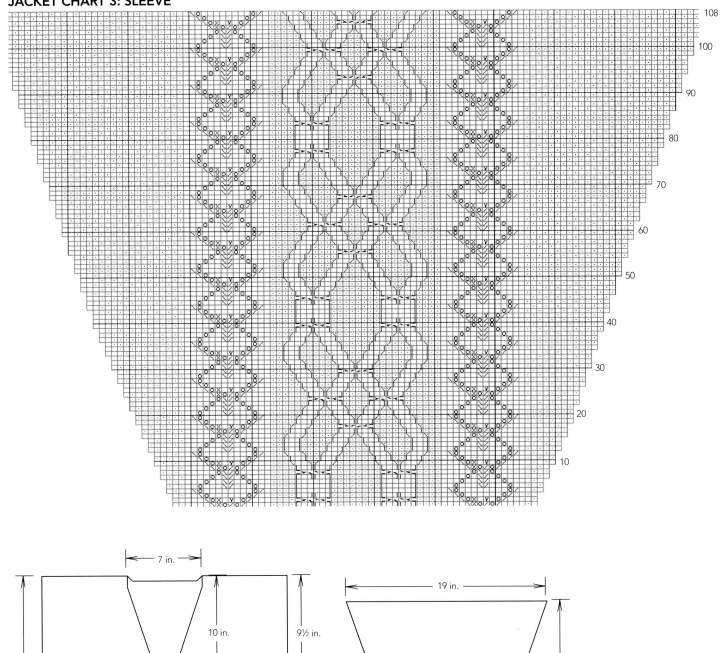

108
100
90
80
70
60
50
40
30
20
10

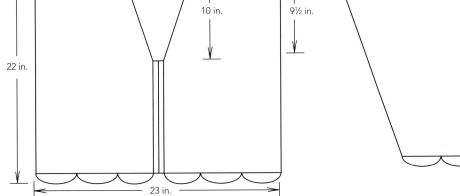

Lisdoonvarna throw

THROW

NEEDLES
- 4.5mm (USA 7) long-length circular needle
- Cable needle
- Large crochet hook

TENSION
24 sts and 26 rows = 4 in. or 10cm over patt

MEASUREMENTS
72 in. (without tassels) by 56 in.

KNITTING THE THROW
Using a 4.5mm circular needle, cast on 340 sts. Foll charts below and on the facing page, work 72 in. back and forth as follows:

ROW 1
Patt 1: sts 1 to 18; patt 2: sts 19 to 32; patt 3: sts 33 to 46; patt 4a: sts 47 to 59; patt 2: sts 60 to 73; patt 5: sts 74 to 101; patt 2: sts 102 to 115; patt 4b: sts 116 to 128; patt 3: sts 129 to 142; patt 2: sts 143 to 156; patt 5: sts 157 to 184; patt 2: sts 185 to 198; patt 3: sts 199 to 212; patt 4a: sts 213 to 225; patt 2: sts 226 to 239; patt 5: sts 240 to 267; patt 2: sts 268 to 281; patt 4b: sts 282 to 294; patt 3: sts 295 to 308; patt 2: sts 309 to 322; patt 1: 323 to 340 (340 sts). Cont in patt as set throughout, rep the last 16 rows of patt 1 every 16 rows, patt 2 every 8 rows, patt 3 every 26 rows, patts 4a and 4b every 4 rows, patt 5 every 38 rows. When work measures 72 in. from cast-on edge, cast off loosely.

FINISHING
To make a fringed edging along cast-on and cast-off edges, use 6 strands of yarn, each 14 in. long, and a large crochet hook. Pull the 6 strands through blanket edge from WS to RS, making a loop on RS. Thread ends of yarn through loop to make tassel approx 5 in. long. Attach tassels every ½ in. across top and bottom edge.

YARN
Rowan Magpie Tweed

Color	Quantity	
Ember 763	25 hanks	x 100g

THROW PATTERN 1

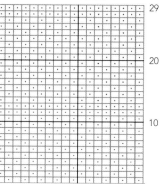

THROW STITCH KEY

Note: Chart starts on purl row (WS), reading from left to right. Read even-numbered rows from right to left.

□	st st—knit on RS and purl on WS
⋅	rev st st—knit on WS and purl on RS
╱	on purl rows, p2tog
╱	on knit rows, k2tog
O	yarn over
X	no st
V	inc 1—(k1, k1 in back loop) in one st
╲	on purl rows, p2tog-b—p1, return it to LH needle, then with point of RH needle pass next st over it and off needle, then sl the st back to RH needle
╲	on knit rows, ssk—sl the first and second sts one at a time as if to knit, then insert point of LH needle into fronts of these 2 sts and knit them tog

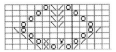

3 over 1 cross—sl 3 sts to cn and hold at front, p1, then k3 from cn

3 over 1 cross—sl 1 st to cn and hold at back, k3, then p1 from cn

(A) 2 over 2 cross—sl 2 sts to cn and hold at front, k2, then k2 from cn

(B) 2 over 2 cross—sl 2 sts to cn and hold at back, k2, then k2 from cn

3 over 3 cross—sl 3 sts to cn and hold at front, k3, then k3 from cn

3 over 3 cross—sl 3 sts to cn and hold at back, k3, then k3 from cn

same as A and B above, worked over 8 sts

on knit rows, right twist—k2tog and leave on needle, insert RH needle between sts just knitted tog and knit first st again, then sl both sts from LH needle
on purl rows, purl right twist—skip 1 st and purl second st, p2tog (skipped st and second st), then sl both sts from needle tog

left twist—skip 1 st and knit second st in back loop, then knit skipped st in front loop and sl both sts from needle tog

THROW PATTERN 4A

THROW PATTERN 4B

THROW PATTERN 5

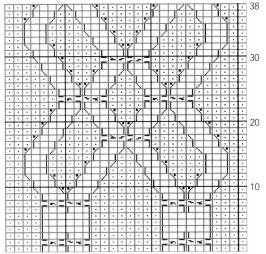

	pattern 1	
	pattern 2	
	pattern 3	
	pattern 4	
	pattern 2	
	pattern 5	
	pattern 2	
	pattern 4	
	pattern 3	
	pattern 2	
	pattern 5	
	pattern 2	
	pattern 3	
	pattern 4	
	pattern 2	
	pattern 5	
	pattern 2	
	pattern 4	
	pattern 3	
	pattern 2	
	pattern 1	

72in.

56 in.

THROW PATTERN 2

THROW PATTERN 3

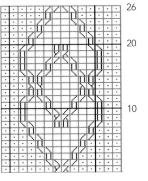

*Lisdoonvarna pillow in colorway 1
(left) and colorway 2*

YARN

Rowan Designer DK

Colorway 1	*Colorway 2*	*Quantity*
Antique Gold 690	Verdigris 685	9 balls x 50g

PILLOW

NEEDLES
- 3.25mm (USA 3)
- 4mm (USA 6)
- Cable needle

TENSION
28 sts and 32 rows = 4 in. or 10cm over patt

MEASUREMENTS
20 in. by 20 in.

BACK
Using 3.25mm needles, cast on 134 sts. Work in moss st as follows:

ROW 1   *K1, p1, rep from * to end.

ROW 2   *P1, k1, rep from * to end.
Rep these 2 rows until work measures 1½ in., then change to 4mm needles. Foll charts 1 and 2 at right, work as follows:

ROW 1   Work 10 sts is moss st, (14 sts from chart 1, 11 sts from chart 2) 4 times across row, 14 sts from chart 1, 10 sts in moss st (134 sts).
Cont as set, rep chart 1 every 26 rows and chart 2 every 4 rows until work measures 18½ in. from cast-on edge.
Change to 3.25mm needles and work a further 1½ in. in moss st. Cast off.

FRONT
Work as for back to end, finishing on a WS row, but do not cast off. Purl 2 rows to form fold at top. Work a further 4 in. in st st and cast off.

FINISHING
Turn down extra 4 in. of front onto inside and oversew in place down side seams (do not sew across width of pillow). Place right sides of pillow together. Using a small, neat backstitch on edge of work, sew around three sides of pillow on WS, leaving top end (with extra 4 in.) open.

TASSELS
Make 4 tassels and attach 1 to each corner of pillow.

PILLOW STITCH KEY
Note: Chart starts on purl row (WS), reading from left to right. Read even-numbered rows from right to left.

☐   st st—knit on RS and purl on WS

⊡   rev st st— knit on WS and purl on RS

on knit rows, right twist—k2tog and leave on needle, insert RH needle between sts just knitted tog and knit the first st again, then sl both sts fom LH needle
on purl rows, purl right twist—skip 1 st and purl second st, p2tog (skipped st and second st), then sl both sts from needle tog

left twist—skip 1 st and knit second st in back loop, then knit skipped st in front loop and sl both sts from needle tog

2 over 2 cross—sl 2 sts to cn and hold at front, k2, then k2 from cn

2 over 2 cross—sl 2 sts to cn and hold at back, k2, then k2 from cn

PILLOW CHART 1

PILLOW CHART 2

SOCKS

NEEDLES
- Set of four 3.25mm (USA 3) double-pointed needles
- Tapestry needle

TENSION
32 sts and 40 rows = 4 in. or 10cm over main patt

MEASUREMENTS
To fit U.S. shoe sizes 5½ to 8½ (English sizes 4 to 7)

MOCK CABLE RIB (IN THE ROUND)
Rnd 1 (RS) *Sl 1, k2, psso, p2, rep from * to end.

Rnd 2 *K1, yo, k1, p2, rep from * to end.

Rnd 3 *K3, p2, rep from * to end.

Rnd 4 *K3, p2, rep from * to end.
Rep these 4 rows.

MOCK CABLE RIB (FOR HEEL)
Rnd 1 (RS) P2, *sl 1, k2, psso, p2, rep from * to end.

Rnd 2 K2, *p1, yo, p1, k2, rep from * to end.

Rnd 3 P2, *k3, p2, rep from * to end.

Rnd 4 K2, *p3, k2, rep from * to end.
Rep these 4 rows.

LACE PATTERN
Rnd 1 (RS) K3, k2tog, yo, k2tog, yo, ssk, k3.

Rnd 2 K2, k2tog, yo, k1, inc 1 in next st, k1, yo, ssk, k2.

Rnd 3 K1, k2tog, yo, k6, yo, ssk, k1.

Rnd 4 K2tog, yo, k8, yo, ssk.

Rnd 5 K1, yo, k3, k2tog, ssk, k3, yo, k1.

Rnd 6 K2, yo, k2, k2tog, ssk, k2, yo, k2.

Rnd 7 K3, yo, k1, k2tog, ssk, k1, yo, k3.

Rnd 8 K4, yo, k2tog, ssk, yo, k4.
Rep these 8 rows.

LEG
Cast on 70 sts using the continental method (see p. 8). Divide the sts onto 3 needles: 20 sts on needle 1 and 25 sts each on needles 2 and 3. (Use the fourth needle to knit.) Join into a rnd, being careful not to twist sts. This join marks the seamline and beg of the rnd.
Work 12 rows in mock cable rib, inc 1 st at beg and end of final rnd (72 sts). Foll lace patt, work a further 56 rows.
Adjust the sts so there are 18 sts on needle 1, 36 sts on needle 2, and 18 sts on needle 3, and so that the seamline is between needles 1 and 3.

DIVIDE FOR HEEL Knit across the first 17 sts on needle 1 with needle 3, inc 1 in last st. There are 37 sts on needle 3 and 36 sts on needle 2 to be held for instep. Turn the work.

NEXT ROW K1tbl, p35, sl 1 with yarn in front. Foll mock cable rib, work 20 rows. K1tbl in first st and sl 1 with yarn in front on every row.

TURN HEEL Beg on a RS row, k1tbl, k18, k2tog tbl, k1, turn. Sl 1 as if to purl, p2, p2tog, p1, turn. *Sl 1 as if to purl, knit to 1 st before the gap, k2tog tbl, k1, turn. Sl 1 as if to purl, purl to 1 st before the gap, p2tog, p1, turn. Rep from * until all sts are worked. There are 19 heel sts.

GUSSETS
Sl 1 as if to purl, k18 heel sts, pick up and k16 sts along right side of heel flap. With an empty needle, pick up and k1tbl at beg of instep sts. Work across instep sts in established patt (rnd 1 of lace patt, starting on sixth st to keep patt correct). Pick up and k1tbl at end of instep sts. With an empty needle, pick up and k16 sts along left side of heel flap, then knit the first 9 sts from heel needle onto this last needle. There are 26 sts on needle 1, 38 instep sts on needle 2, and 25 sts on needle 3.

YARN
Rowan 4-ply Botany

Colorway 1	Colorway 2	Quantity
Redwood 549	Nettle 551	2 balls x 50g

SHAPE GUSSETS: RND 1 Beg at center back heel, knit to 3 sts from the end of needle 1, k2tog, k1. P2tog at beg of needle 2, then work across instep in established patt to last 2 sts, p2tog. K1, ssk at beg of needle 3. Knit to end of rnd.

RND 2 Work in established patt, working instep in lace patt and rest in st st.

RND 3 Work dec at end of needle 1 and at beg of needle 3 only. (Omit the dec on needle 2.) Rep these last 2 rnds a total of 6 times, then rep rnd 3 twice. Now 69 sts rem—17 sts on needle 1, 36 instep sts on needle 2, and 16 sts on needle 3. Cont in lace patt bordered by st st for 6 in. from start of gusset (or until sock reaches 2 in. less than the desired length). End with a full rep of the lace patt and dec 1 st at end of needle 2 on last row. Transfer this last st to needle 3. There are now 17 sts on needle 1, 34 sts on needle 2, and 17 sts on needle 3.

TOE

Work in moss st (rnd 1: k1, p1; rnd 2: p1, k1; rep these 2 rnds).

RND 1 Work to 3 sts from end of needle 1, k2tog, k1. K1, ssk at beg of needle 2, work to 3 sts from end of needle 2, k2tog, k1. K1, ssk at beg of needle 3, work to end.

RND 2 Work to 2 sts from end of needle 1, k2. K2 at beg of needle 2. K2 at beg of needle 3, work to end.
Rep these 2 rnds until 32 sts rem. Work dec every rnd until 8 sts rem. Cut yarn, leaving an 8-in. tail. Thread the yarn through the tapestry needle, draw the end through the rem sts, and pull snugly. Weave the ends into the inside of the sock.

DAJAN

JACKET

WAISTCOAT

SLIPPER
SOCKS

SERAPÉ

The sumptuously embroidered indigo wing-sleeved dress, or *thob*, shown above was part of a bride's trousseau in Beit Dajan in Southern Palestine in the 1930s. The lines of stylized inverted cypress trees and triangles that decorate the back skirt panel, or *shinyar*, are the hallmark of the village, declaring the wealth and marital status of the wearer. The Syrian red-and-gold-striped Atlas satin at the yoke and on the sleeves, which is not shown, symbolizes the bride's passage from virgin to married woman. As always in Palestinian costume, great emphasis is placed on the design of the seams, which here have been embellished with alternating red, magenta, and orange silk. The changing colors are said to deflect and confuse the evil eye.

In the Dajan jacket and socks, I have used the chevron design from the bottom of the dress as the main pattern, converting the design into a monotone textured stitch and enlarging the motif to fill the width of the piece. I love the dress's embroidered seams and have incorporated this idea also. I wanted to keep the knitting simple, so

I've used an easy slipstitch pattern for the hem and bands of the jacket and the top of the socks. This creates the illusion of fairisle while being knitted in stripes. Four pairs of horn teardrop buttons, with their inlays of copper triangles symbolizing protection and fertility, complete the jacket.

In the Dajan waistcoat, I have used the decorated seams as an allover design, interspersing these seams, knitted in an interesting fagot stitch, with the stripes from the Atlas satin. The vest is finished with a hand of Fatima button, another potent symbol used to ward off evil.

In the Dajan serapé, I have enlarged the Atlas satin stripes in one panel and worked the other panel solid to stress the striped theme. I'm pleased with the rib stitch that is used throughout, and it's easy to knit, is beautifully substantial, and makes the garment reversible.

All of the pieces in this chapter indulge my love of mixing texture and color and are easy to knit for anyone who is competent in the basics.

JACKET

NEEDLES
- 4mm (USA 6)
- 5mm (USA 8)
- 4mm (USA 6) circular
- Tapestry needle

BUTTONS
Eight 32mm teardrops

TENSION
17 sts and 25 rows = 4 in. or 10cm over patt

SIZE
One size to fit 34-in. to 44-in. bust
See diagram on p. 89 for finished knitted measurements.

YARN
Rowan Magpie Aran

Key	Colorway 1	Colorway 2	Quantity	
A	Squirrel 772	Cork 309	10 hanks	x 100g
B	Sea Lord 608	Admiral 504	3 hanks	x 100g
C	Comanche 503	Neptune 612	3 hanks	x 100g

Previous page: Dajan jacket in colorway 2

BACK
Using 4mm needles and col B, cast on 127 sts. Work in garter slipstitch as follows:

ROW 1 (RS) Using col B, knit.

ROW 2 Using col B, knit.

ROW 3 Using col C, k1, *sl 1 purlwise, k1, rep from * to end.

ROW 4 Using col C, k1, *yarn forward, sl 1 purlwise, yarn back, k1, rep from * to end. Rep these 4 rows until work measures 2½ in., dec 1 st in final st (126 sts). Change to 5mm needles and work as follows:

ROW 1 Using col B, sl 1 purlwise, k2tog, yo, k2. Using col A, (k5, p1, k1, p1) 7 times, k2tog, yo, k2, (p1, k1, p1, k5) 7 times. Using col B, k2tog, yo, k2, sl 1 purlwise.

ROW 2 Using col B, p1, k2tog, yo, k2. Using col A, (p4, k1, p1, k1, p1) 7 times, k2tog, yo, k2, (p1, k1, p1, k1, p4) 7 times. Using col B, k2tog, yo, k2, p1.

ROW 3 Using col B, sl 1 purlwise, k2tog, yo, k2. Using col A (k3, p1, k1, p1, k2) 7 times, k2tog, yo, k2, (k2, p1, k1, p1, k3) 7 times. Using col B, k2tog, yo, k2, sl 1 purlwise.

ROW 4 Using col B, p1, k2tog, yo, k2. Using col A, (p2, k1, p1, k1, p3) 7 times, k2tog, yo, k2, (p3, k1, p1, k1, p2) 7 times. Using col B, k2tog, yo, k2, p1.

ROW 5 Using col B, sl 1 purlwise, k2tog, yo, k2. Using col A, (k1, p1, k1, p1, k4) 7 times, k2tog, yo, k2, (k4, p1, k1, p1, k1) 7 times. Using col B, k2tog, yo, k2, sl 1 purlwise.

ROW 6 Using col B, p1, k2tog, yo, k2. Using col A, (k1, p1, k1, p5) 7 times, k2tog, yo, k2, (p5, k1, p1, k1) 7 times. Using col B, k2tog, yo, k2, p1.

ROW 7 Using col B, sl 1 purlwise, k2tog, yo, k2. Using col A, (k1, p1, k5, p1) 7 times, k2tog, yo, k2, (p1, k5, p1, k1) 7 times. Using col B, k2tog, yo, k2, sl 1 purlwise.

ROW 8 Using col B, p1, k2tog, yo, k2. Using col A, (k1, p5, k1, p1) 7 times, k2tog, yo, k2, (p1, k1, p5, k1) 7 times. Using col B, k2tog, yo, k2, p1. Rep these 8 rows until work measures 34½ in. from cast-on edge and ends on a WS row.

SHAPE SHOULDER AND NECKLINE Place 9 sts on a st holder and work to end of row. Rep on next row. Place 10 sts on a st holder and work to end of row. Rep on next 2 rows. Place 10 sts on a st holder, work 22 sts, place the next 24 sts on a st holder, and work rem 22 sts. Place 10 sts on a st holder, work 10 sts, k2tog, then turn. Working sides separately, p2tog and work to end. Leave rem 10 sts on a st holder. Rejoin yarn at other side neck edge, k2tog, and work to end. Place 10 sts at beg of next row on a st holder, work to last 2 sts, p2tog. Work 1 row, then leave rem 10 sts on a st holder.

RIGHT FRONT

Using 4mm needles and col B, cast on 53 sts. Work in garter slipstitch as before for 2½ in., ending on a WS row.
Change to 5mm needles and cont to end in patt as follows:

ROW 1 (RS) Using col A, (p1, k1, p1, k5) 6 times. Using col B, k2tog, yo, k2, sl 1 st purlwise.

ROW 2 Using col B, p1, k2tog, yo, k2. Using col A, (p4, k1, p1, k1, p1) 6 times.

ROW 3 Using col A, (k2, p1, k1, p1, k3) 6 times. Using col B, k2tog, yo, k2, sl 1 st purlwise.

ROW 4 Using col B, p1, k2tog, yo, k2. Using col A, (p2, k1, p1, k1, p3) 6 times.

ROW 5 Using col A, (k4, p1, k1, p1, k1) 6 times. Using col B, k2tog, yo, k2, sl 1 st purlwise.

ROW 6 Using col B, p1, k2tog, yo, k2. Using col A, (k1, p1, k1, p5) 6 times.

ROW 7 Using col A, (p1, k5, p1, k1) 6 times. Using col B, k2tog, yo, k2, sl 1 st purlwise.

ROW 8 Using col B, p1, k2tog, yo, k2. Using col A, (k1, p5, k1, p1) 6 times.
Rep these 8 rows until work measures 33½ in. from cast-on edge and ends on a WS row.

SHAPE NECKLINE Dec 1 st at beg (neck edge) of next and every alt row 4 times. Place 9 sts on a st holder and work to end. Work 1 row. Place an additional 10 sts on a st holder and work to end. Work 1 row. Rep the last 2 rows twice more, then leave rem 10 sts on a st holder.

Dajan jacket in colorway 1

LEFT FRONT

Using 4mm needles and col B, cast on 53 sts. Work in garter slipstitch as before for 2½ in., ending on a WS row.

Change to 5mm needles and cont to end in patt as follows:

ROW 1   Using col B, sl 1 purlwise, k2tog, yo, k2. Using col A, (k5, p1, k1, p1) 6 times.

ROW 2   Using col A, (p1, k1, p1, k1, p4) 6 times. Using col B, k2tog, yo, k2, p1.

ROW 3   Using col B, sl 1 purlwise, k2tog, yo, k2. Using col A, (k3, p1, k1, p1, k2) 6 times.

ROW 4   Using col A, (p3, k1, p1, k1, p2) 6 times. Using col B, k2tog, yo, k2, p1.

ROW 5   Using col B, sl 1 purlwise, k2tog, yo, k2. Using col A, (k1, p1, k1, p1, k4) 6 times.

ROW 6   Using col A, (p5, k1, p1, k1) 6 times. Using col B, k2tog, yo, k2, p1.

ROW 7   Using col B, sl 1 purlwise, k2tog, yo, k2. Using col A, (k1, p1, k5, p1) 6 times.

ROW 8   Using col A, (p1, k1, p5, k1) 6 times. Using col B, k2tog, yo, k2, p1.
Rep these 8 rows until work measures 33½ in. and ends on a RS row.

SHAPE NECKLINE   Dec 1 st at beg (neck edge) of next and every alt row 4 times. Place 9 sts on a st holder and work to end. Work 1 row. Place 10 sts on a st holder and work to end. Work 1 row. Rep the last 2 rows twice more, then leave rem 10 sts on a st holder.

SLEEVES

Using col C and 4mm circular needle, cast on 61 sts. Work in garter slipstitch for 5 in., working back and forth, not in the round. Work rows 1 and 2 in col C and rows 3 and 4 in col B. Inc 1 st in last row (62 sts).

When work measures 5 in. and ends on a WS row, break yarn and slide the work to the other end of the needle. Cont to knit using col C, rejoining yarn at other end. With WS facing, knit in k1, p1 rib for another 5 in. Change to 5mm needles and cont in patt using col A to end as follows:

ROW 1 (RS)   K2, p1, k1, p1, (k5, p1, k1, p1) 3 times, k2tog, yo, k2, (p1, k1, p1, k5) 3 times, p1, k1, p1, k2 (62 sts).

ROW 2   P1, k1, p1, k1, p1, (p4, k1, p1, k1, p1) 3 times, k2tog, yo, k2, (p1, k1, p1, k1, p4) 3 times, p1, k1, p1, k1, p1.

ROW 3   P1, k1, p1, k2, (k3, p1, k1, p1, k2) 3 times, k2tog, yo, k2, (k2, p1, k1, p1, k3) 3 times, k2, p1, k1, p1.

ROW 4   P1, k1, p3, (p2, k1, p1, k1, p3) 3 times, k2tog, yo, k2, (p3, k1, p1, k1, p2) 3 times, p3, k1, p1.

ROW 5   P1, k4, (k1, p1, k1, p1, k4) 3 times, k2tog, yo, k2, (k4, p1, k1, p1, k1) 3 times, k4, p1.

ROW 6   P5, (k1, p1, k1, p5) 3 times, k2tog, yo, k2, (p5, k1, p1, k1) 3 times, p5.

ROW 7   K4, p1, (k1, p1, k5, p1) 3 times, k2tog, yo, k2, (p1, k5, p1, k1) 3 times, p1, k4.

ROW 8   P3, k1, p1, (k1, p5, k1, p1) 3 times, k2tog, yo, k2, (p1, k1, p5, k1) 3 times, p1, k1, p3.
Rep these 8 rows to end of sleeve.

At the same time, when work measures 10 in. from cast-on edge, inc 1 st at both ends of every foll fourth row 18 times (98 sts), keeping patt correct to edges of sleeves as you inc. Cont until work measures 22½ in. from cast-on edge, then cast off.

BUTTON BAND

Using col C and 4mm needles, cast on 11 sts. Work in garter slipstitch using col C for rows 1 and 2 and col B for rows 3 and 4. Cont until band fits left front when slightly stretched. Slipstitch into place.

Mark the position of 8 buttons as follows:
1—¾ in. from top
2—2¾ in. from top
3—7¾ in. from top
4—9¾ in. from top
5—14¾ in. from top
6—16¾ in. from top
7—21¾ in. from top
8—23¾ in. from top
This leaves the lowest button 9¼ in. from bottom of jacket.

BUTTONHOLE BAND

Using col C and 4mm needles, cast on 23 sts.
Work as for button band in garter slipstitch in
cols C and B, with the addition of 8 buttonholes
to correspond with markers. Make buttonholes
on RS rows as follows:

BUTTONHOLE ROW   Patt 3, cast off 3, patt
to end.

NEXT ROW   Patt across row, casting on the
3 sts in place of those cast off.
Slipstitch band into place.

COLLAR

Join shoulders using Kitchener st (see p. 9)
as follows:
With RS facing and using col A, place the 49 sts
from back shoulder on one needle and the
49 sts from front shoulder on another. Hold the
two needles parallel and close together with the
yarn coming from the right-hand end of the
back needle (if there is no yarn there, then
attach here securely). Leaving enough yarn to
join shoulder (at least 60 in.), thread the yarn
onto a tapestry needle. Work Kitchener st until
all sts are used up. Weave in end and snip off.
Join the other shoulder in the same way.
Using col C and 4mm needles, with RS facing,
and starting 1 in. into button band (1 in. without
collar), pick up and knit 6 sts to end of button
band; 18 sts up to shoulder; 4 sts down back
neck; 22 sts from st holder at center back; 4 sts
up other side back neck; 18 sts down other side
front neck to buttonhole band; and 6 sts across
the first inch of buttonhole band, leaving 4 in.
without collar (78 sts). Work 4 rows in k1, p1 rib.
Working in garter stitch (all rows knit), work a
further 20 rows as follows:

ROW 1   Sl 1, k1, p1, knit to last 3 sts, p1, k1,
k1tbl.

ROW 2   Sl 1, p1, k1, knit into front and back of
next st to make a st, knit to last 4 sts, knit into
front and back of next st to make a st, k1, p1,
k1tbl.
Cont in this way, working 3 sts in rib at each
edge of collar, working garter stitch between,

and inc 1 st at each end of every alt row.
Change to col B, rep rows 1 and 2 twice, then
cast off loosely.

FINISHING

Use a small, neat backstitch for all seams unless
otherwise stated. Find center of top of sleeve
and place at shoulder seam. Insert sleeves. Join
side and sleeve seams in one line down to 10 in.
from bottom on side seams. Turn back cuffs
onto RS and slipstitch neatly into place. Attach
8 buttons on button band directly opposite
buttonholes, keeping patt correct across front
of jacket.

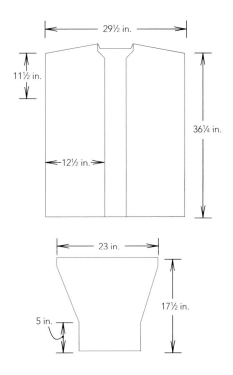

WAISTCOAT

NEEDLES
- 4mm (USA 6)
- 3.25mm (USA 3) crochet hook

BUTTONS
One hand-shaped 40mm by 20mm

TENSION
23 sts and 40 rows = 4 in. over moss st

SIZE
One size to fit 34-in. to 40-in. bust
See diagram on p. 92 for finished knitted measurements.

STITCH NOTE
Slip the first stitch and knit into the back of the last stitch on every row. This eliminates curl and makes finishing easier, as the resulting notches can be matched.

MOSS STITCH
Row 1 (RS) *K1, p1, rep from * to end.

Row 2 *P1, k1, rep from * to end.
Rep these 2 rows.

YARN
Rowan Designer DK (cols A and E in colorway 1; cols C and F in colorway 2); Rowan Lightweight DK (cols C and D in colorway 1); Rowan Fine Cotton Chenille (cols B and F in colorway 1; cols B and E in colorway 2); Rowan DK Marl (cols A and D in colorway 2)

Key	Colorway 1	Colorway 2	Quantity	
A	Rust 663		3 balls	x 50g
		Licorice 825	3 hanks	x 50g
B	Privet 410	Ruby 407	2 balls	x 50g
C	Wine 637		4 hanks	x 25g
		Cinnamon 691	2 balls	x 50g
D	Dark Blue 54		8 hanks	x 25g
		Pastille 824	4 hanks	x 50g
E	Verdigris 661	Privet 410	3 balls	x 50g
F	Plum 409	Verdigris 661	2 balls	x 50g

CRESTED GARTER STITCH
Row 1 (WS) Knit.

Row 2 Knit every stitch as follows: Insert the needle knitwise into the stitch. Throw the yarn under and over the right needle, then under and over the left needle, and under the right needle again, as shown in the left illustration below. Slightly open the needles and draw through the loop singly, as shown in the right illustration below, and slip it off the needle, together with the stitch and second throw.

CRESTED GARTER STITCH

PATTERN 1 (25 ROWS)
Starting on RS

Rows 1 to 7 Moss st in col A.

Rows 8 to 11 Moss st in col B.

Rows 12 to 14 Crested garter st in col C.

Rows 15 to 18 Moss st in col B.

Rows 19 to 25 Moss st in col A.

PATTERN 2 (43 ROWS)
Starting on WS

Rows 1 to 11 Moss st in col D.

Rows 12 to 17 Moss st in col E.

Rows 18 to 20 Moss st in col F.

Rows 21 to 23 Crested garter st in col C.

Rows 24 to 26 Moss st in col F.

Rows 27 to 32 Moss st in col E.

Rows 33 to 43 Moss st in col D.

Dajan waistcoat in colorway 1
(left) and colorway 2

CENTER BACK PANEL (45 ROWS)

Starting on RS

Rows 1 to 14 As pattern 1, rows 1 to 14.

Rows 15 to 21 Moss st in col E.

Rows 22 to 24 Crested garter st in col F.

Rows 25 to 31 Moss st in col E.

Rows 32 to 45 As pattern 1, rows 12 to 25.

WAISTCOAT (ONE PIECE)

Using col A and 4mm needles, cast on 100 sts.
Work 453 rows as follows:
*Pattern 1, pattern 2, rep from * 3 times
(204 rows), center back panel (45 rows),
**pattern 2, pattern 1, rep from ** 3 times
(204 rows).
At the same time, work shapings:

RIGHT FRONT NECK

ROWS 2 TO 30 Cast on 4 sts at end of row 2
and every alt row 15 times (160 sts).

RIGHT ARMHOLE

ROW 71 Cast off 34 sts at beg of row.

ROWS 72 TO 89 Dec 1 st at end of row 72 and
every alt row 9 times (117 sts).

ROWS 90 TO 104 Dec 1 st at armhole edge on
every row 15 times (102 sts).

ROWS 105 TO 120 Work without shaping in
patt as set.

ROWS 121 TO 135 Inc 1 st at armhole edge on
every row 15 times (117 sts).

ROWS 136 TO 152 Inc 1 st at end of row 136
and every alt row 9 times (126 sts).

ROW 153 Work in patt as set.

ROW 154 Cast on 34 sts at end of row (160 sts).

BACK NECK

ROWS 197 TO 201 Dec 1 st at beg of row 197
and at beg of every alt row 3 times (157 sts).

ROWS 253 TO 257 Inc 1 st at beg of row 249
and at beg of every alt row 3 times (160 sts).

LEFT ARMHOLE

ROWS 300 TO 383 Work as rows 71 to 154 for
right armhole.

LEFT FRONT NECK

ROWS 423 TO 452 Cast off 4 sts at beg of
row 423 and every alt row 15 times (100 sts).
Work 1 row, then cast off evenly and fairly
loosely, so that cast-on and cast-off edges are
same tension.

FINISHING

Join shoulder seams using a small, neat
backstitch on edge of work.
Note: For double crochet, make 1 st for every st
made horizontally and every other row vertically.
Rows are marked by the notches made by
slipping the first st, etc. (1 notch every 2 rows).

ARMBANDS AND BOTTOM EDGE Using a
3.25mm crochet hook, work 1 row of double
crochet in each of cols F, E, and D around
armholes and bottom edge. **Note:** Start
armholes at underarm, *not* at shoulder seam.

NECKBAND Starting at bottom of right front
(including crocheted edge) and finishing at
bottom of left front, work 2 rows of double
crochet around neckline in col F, 1 row of double
crochet in col E, and finish with 2 rows of double
crochet in col D.
At the same time, on col E row, work buttonhole on right front band by skipping 3 sts and
making 3 chains. Mark position of buttonhole
on portion of band already knitted after first
2 rows where the V-neck comes together.

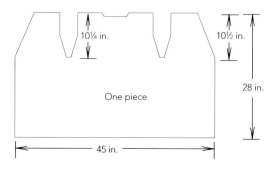

SLIPPER SOCKS

NEEDLES
- Set of 5 double-pointed 4mm (USA 6)
- Set of 5 double-pointed 5mm (USA 8)
- 5mm crochet hook
- Tapestry needle

TENSION
17 sts and 25 rows = 4 in. or 10cm over patt

SIZE
To fit U.S. sizes 5½ to 8½ (English sizes 4 to 7)

INTARSIA KNITTING IN THE ROUND
As the yarn will be on the WS of a color block at the end of each round, turn the work at the end of each color block and purl back to the beg of the block (as if knitting back and forth), twisting the yarns at the end of each block. Slip these stitches on RS rounds.

Dajan slipper socks in colorway 1 (left) and colorway 2

FIRST SOCK
Using col A and 5mm needles, cast on 4 sts using straight wrap method (see p. 7). Working back and forth, work 8 rows in st st.

Begin knitting in the round. At this point there will be a needle at each end of the strip. Rotate work to side edge of knitted strip. With the third needle, pick up and k4 sts across this edge—one st each in the middle of the st at the end of every other row. Rotate and work across the initial cast-on sts. Rotate and pick up and k4 sts along the final edge (16 sts).

The work is now in a rectangle. Reposition the sts to divide in the middle of the cast-on sts at each side and in the middle of the top and bottom sts. Designate position in the middle of the end sts (those which are picked up) as the beg of each rnd.

YARN
Rowan Magpie Aran

Key		Colorway 1	Colorway 2	Quantity	
☐	A	Comanche 503	Neptune 612	1 hank	x 100g
O	B	Squirrel 772	Cork 309	1 hank	x 100g
X	C	Sea Lord 608	Admiral 504	1 hank	x 100g

SLIPPER SOCKS STITCH KEY

·	purl in col A
●	purl in col B
⋈	purl in col C
S	sl 1 st purlwise
✳	yarn back, sl 1 st knitwise, yarn forward

SLIPPER SOCKS CHART 1

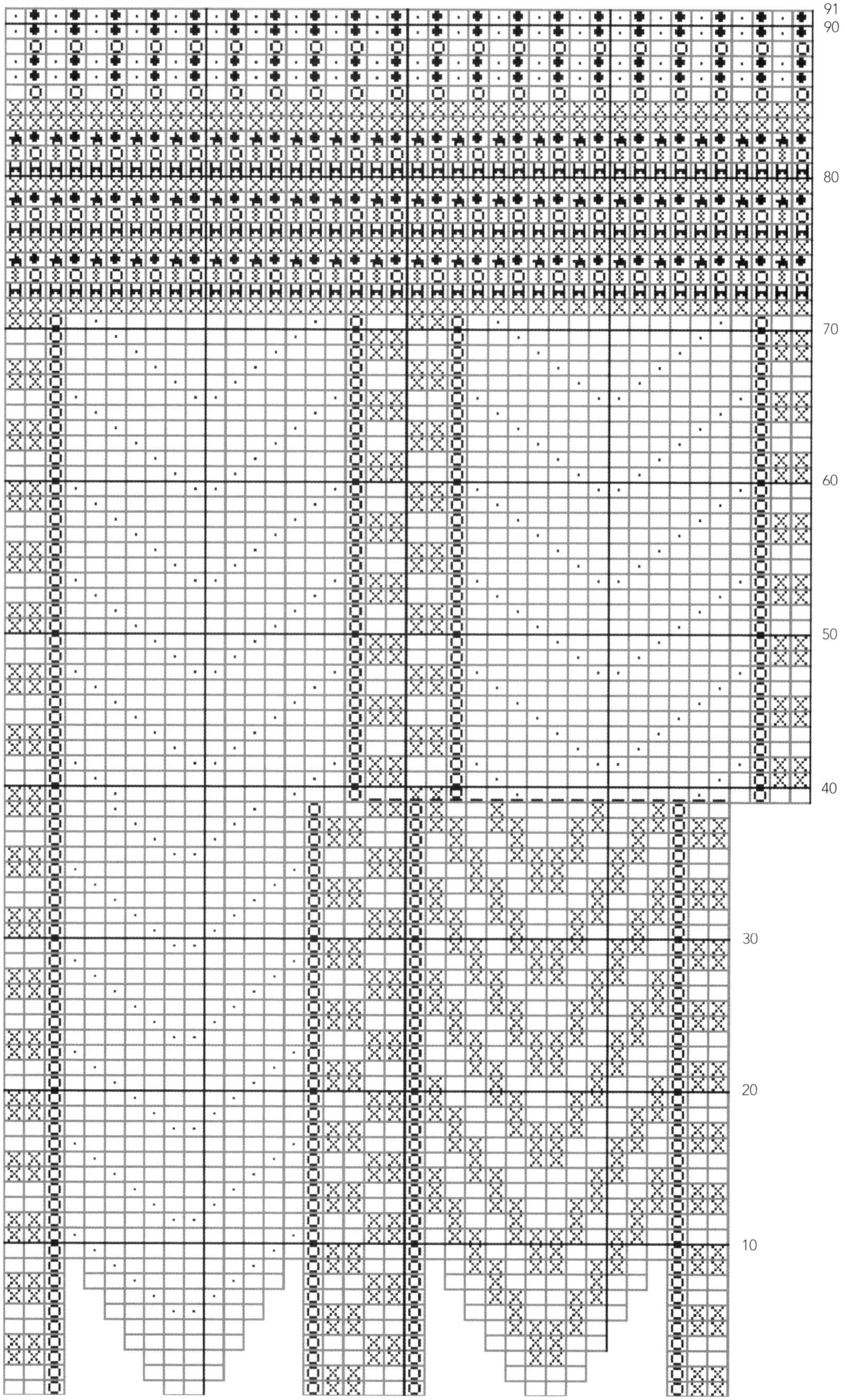

TOE SHAPING

Note: As you are working in the round in st st, all rows are knit rows and chart is read from right to left on every rnd.

Foll chart 1 on the facing page, work 91 rnds, working toe shaping on rnds 2, 4, 6, 8, and 10 as follows:

Work 3 sts, make 1 st (insert LH needle from back to front into strand between last st worked and next st on LH needle, knit through front loop), work 2 sts, make 1 st, work 6 sts, make 1 st, work 2 sts, make 1 st, work 3 sts.

Cont on alt rnds, inc 4 times in each rnd 3 sts in from edge of toe.

Insert 1 row of waste yarn over the 18 sts indicated on chart between rnds 39 and 40.

RND 40 Pick up sts from waste yarn and inc 1 st between sts 3 and 4, 15 and 16, 21 and 22, and 33 and 34 (40 sts).

Note: Rnds 86 to 91 inclusive are worked in braid patt as follows:

RND 86 Foll chart 1, knit.

RND 87 Foll chart 1, purl, always bringing the next col to be used *over* the top of the last col used.

RND 88 Foll chart 1, purl, always bringing the next col to be used *under* the last col used.

RNDS 89 TO 91 Rep rnds 86 to 88.
Cast off loosely using both yarns.

WORK HEEL

To insert the heel, pick up 38 sts using 4mm needles for first rnd. Pick up the 36 sts from the waste yarn plus 2 extra sts, 1 on each side in gap between needles. Dec the extra 2 sts on first rnd (36 sts).

Change to 5mm needles. Foll chart 2 at right, work the heel, dec on rnds 9, 11, 13, 14, 15, and 16 as follows:

K3, sl 1, k1, psso, k8, k2tog, k6, sl 1, k1, psso, k8, k2tog, k3.

Cont with dec as set, keeping dec 3 sts in from side panels on every dec rnd. To close the heel, thread yarn through all sts using a tapestry needle and draw up and fasten off securely on WS.

SECOND SOCK

Work as for first sock, but work sts 19 to 36 first, then sts 1 to 18 inclusive, so sole patt will be on the left and the join will be on the inside of each sock.

SLIPPER SOCKS CHART 2

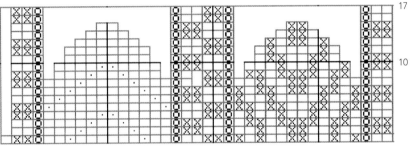

SERAPÉ

NEEDLES
- 4mm (USA 6)
- Tapestry needle

TENSION
28 sts and 34 rows = 4 in. over rib patt

MEASUREMENTS
67 in. by 44 in.

STITCH NOTE
Slip the first st and knit into the back of the last st on every row. This eliminates curl and makes finishing easier as the resulting notches can be matched.

RIB PATTERN
Row 1 *K3, p3, rep from * to end.
Row 2 *K1, p1, rep from * to end.
Rep rows 1 and 2.

YARN
Rowan Designer DK (cols A, B, and C in colorways 1 and 2); Rowan Chunky Chenille (col D in colorways 1 and 2); Rowan Kid Silk (colorway 3)

Key	Colorway 1	Colorway 2	Colorway 3	Quantity	
A	Damson 659	Black 062		24 balls	x 50g
			It. Brown 972	39 balls	x 25g
B	Cinnamon 691	Rust 663		5 balls	x 50g
			Goat Brown 994 (cols B & D)	8 balls	x 25g
C	Lovat Green 685	Taupe 695		3 balls	x 50g
			Turnip 997	3 balls	x 25g
D	Forest Green 362	Elephant 348		1 hank	x 100g

FIRST PIECE
Using 4mm needles and col A, cast on 156 sts. Work in rib patt for 572 rows, then cast off.

SECOND PIECE
Using 4mm needles and col A, cast on 156 sts. Work in rib patt for 572 rows in the foll striped patt:

ROWS 1 TO 36   Rib patt in col A (36 rows).

ROWS 37 TO 58   Rib patt in col B (22 rows).

ROWS 59 TO 68   Rib patt in col C (10 rows).

ROWS 69 TO 114   Rib patt in col A (46 rows).

ROWS 115 TO 504   Rep rows 37 to 114 5 times (390 rows).

ROWS 505 TO 536   Rep rows 37 to 68 (32 rows).

ROWS 537 TO 572   Rib patt in col A (36 rows). Cast off.

FINISHING
Using col A and an invisible slipstitch seam, join serapé down center from row 302 to row 572 inclusive.

BLANKET STITCH   Working from left to right with tapestry needle threaded with col D, attach yarn at center back seam at bottom edge and hold the working thread below the edge of the serapé with the left thumb. Insert the needle no more than ½ in. above the edge and bring it out below the edge but above the working thread. Tighten the loop thus formed without drawing up the edge of the serapé. Cont around the entire serapé, setting the sts no more than ½ in. apart.

Dajan serapé in colorway 3 (left) and colorway 1

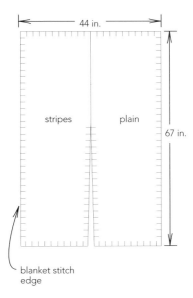

44 in.

stripes | plain

67 in.

blanket stitch edge

MAYA

JACKET

THROW

PILLOW

HAT

The sumptuous Guatemalan *huipil*, or woman's blouse, shown above was made by the Ixil people who live in Nebaj in the Quiche district. The dazzling embroidered weaving, announcing the wearer's village and marital status, still uses ancient earth-mystery imagery, traceable to the sun-worshiping Mayan civilization more than 3,000 years ago. The hummingbirds represent good and evil and the diamonds the four cardinal points of the world. The sacred Mayan tree is at the center. Despite centuries of repression, the Guatemalan people continue their craft tradition, and their textiles offer us a glimpse of the cultural and historical identity of a unique people.

In the Maya jacket, throw, and pillow, I have tried to capture the magical colors, stripes, and geometric shapes of the *huipil*. The jacket's godet stripes are great fun and ever so easy to wear. As I love to add texture, I've worked every alternate stripe in moss stitch and added the beautiful brass sun buttons to complete the Mayan theme. It's an easy intarsia knit, as is the throw, which has the bonus of keeping you so

warm while you knit that you can turn off the heat! If intarsia knitting is too challenging for you, the throw would also look fabulous with stripes throughout and finished with an original combination of tassels and fringes. You could really go to town on these—a riot of multicolored tassel jewels would make a fabulous Mayan edging. Although the pillow is intrinsically a more demanding knit, the reverse side is moss stitch so you will complete your project before you know it. Again, this is a great pillow for individual expressions of color. As long as the colors are strong and vibrant, it really doesn't matter if they appear to clash—practically anything goes in this piece.

The felted Maya hat is composed of nine sun-ray stripes, which can be colored to match the Maya jacket or another favorite sweater. Its versatile shape allows you to wear it either fully rolled as a beret or loosely rolled to create a more eccentric out-line. I promise that you can virtually feel the sun beating down when you knit one of these Mayan-inspired designs!

JACKET

NEEDLES

- 3mm (USA 2) circular
- 3.75mm (USA 5) circular
- 3.25mm (USA 3)
- 3.75mm (USA 5)

BUTTONS

Six 20mm

TENSION

24 sts and 32 rows = 4 in. or 10cm over patt

SIZE

One size to fit 34-in. to 42-in. bust
See diagram on p. 103 for finished knitted measurements.

YARN

Rowan Lightweight DK

Key	Colorway 1	Colorway 2	Quantity	
A	Blue 53	Caramel 603	9 hanks	x 25g
B	Green 91	Burgundy 132	7 hanks	x 25g
C	Plum 70	Rust 27	7 hanks	x 25g
D	Dusty Purple 652	Teal Blue 54	10 hanks	x 25g
E	Cinnamon 136	Purple 99	3 hanks	x 25g
F	Magenta 46	Magenta 46	2 hanks	x 25g
G	Dark Blue 108	Green 91	2 hanks	x 25g
H	Rust 27	Cinnamon 136	2 hanks	x 25g
I	Pale Green 133	Turquoise 125	1 hank	x 25g
J	Teal Blue 54	Aquamarine 90	2 hanks	x 25g
K	Purple 99	Gold 72	2 hanks	x 25g

Previous page: Maya hat and jacket in colorway 2 (left) and colorway 1

BACK

Using 3mm circular needle and col D, cast on 262 sts. Working back and forth, begin two-col striped rib as follows:

ROW 1 (RS) *Using col D, k2. Using col A, p2. Rep from * to last 2 sts. Using col D, k2.

ROW 2 *Using col D, p2. Using col A, k2. Rep from * to last 2 sts. Using col D, p2.
Rep these 2 rows until rib measures 1¼ in. from cast-on edge and ends on WS row.
Change to 3.75mm circular needle. Beg with a knit row, foll chart 1 on p. 102 as follows:

ROWS 1 TO 16 Sl 1 st, work the 52 sts of chart twice, work the first 26 sts, work the 52 sts twice, work the first 26 sts, k1tbl (262 sts).

ROWS 17 ONWARD Start to fill in the stripes between the diamonds (beg with sts 13 and 14, 39 and 40, etc., and inc the stripe sts every row until the stripe covers the full 26 sts) in the foll col sequence across row:
A D B D C A D B D C.
Cont until all 205 rows have been completed, ending with a RS row.

DEC Work dec on col D stripe as follows:
On knit rows—work to edge of stripe, ssk. Work to last 2 sts at other side of stripe and k2tog. Work dec on cols A, B, and C stripes as follows:
On knit rows—work to last 2 sts before the 2 sts of rev st st, k2tog, patt 2 sts, then ssk.
When 205 rows are completed, foll chart 2 on p. 103 for rem 86 sts, starting with a WS row.
Cast off on row 234.

JACKET STITCH KEY

⊡   rev st st—using col for that particular stripe, purl on RS and knit on WS

Maya jacket in colorway 1

JACKET CHART 1: BACK AND FRONT

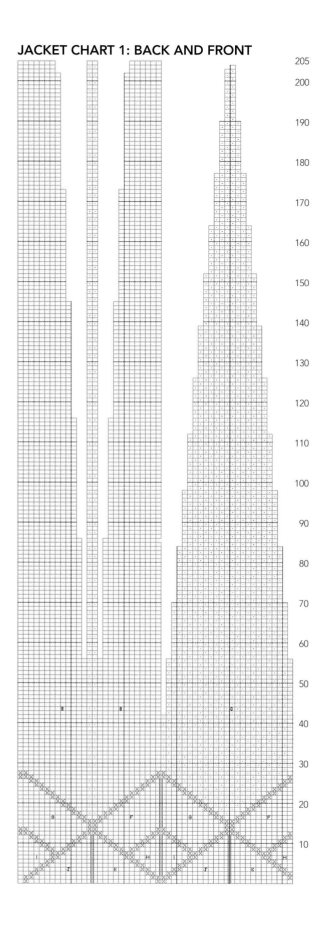

LEFT FRONT

Using 3.25mm needles and col D, cast on 131 sts. Work striped rib as follows:

ROW 1 (RS) Using col D, k1. *Using col D, k2. Using col A, p2. Rep from * to last 2 sts. Using col D, k2.

ROW 2 *Using col D, p2. Using col A, k2. Rep from * to last 3 sts. Using col D, p3.
Rep these 2 rows until rib measures 1¼ in. from cast-on edge and ends on a WS row.
Change to 3.75mm needles. Foll chart 1, beg with a knit row, work as follows until 165 rows are completed: Sl 1 st, work the 52 sts twice, work the first 26 sts (131 sts). From row 17, work stripes in the foll col sequence: A D B D C.

SHAPE NECKLINE Dec 1 st at beg (neck edge) of next and every foll third row at neck edge until 24 sts rem.
At the same time, when chart row 205 is completed, foll chart 2 and work to row 233. Cast off.

RIGHT FRONT

Using 3.25mm needles and col D, cast on 131 sts. Work striped rib as follows:

ROW 1 (RS) *Using col D, k2. Using col A, p2. Rep from * to last 3 sts. Using col D, k3.

ROW 2 Using col D, p1. *Using col D, p2. Using col A, k2. Rep from * to last 2 sts. Using col D, p2.
Rep these 2 rows until rib measures 1¼ in. from cast-on edge and ends on WS row.
Change to 3.75mm needles. Foll chart 1, beg with a knit row, work as for left front, working stripes from row 17 in the same col sequence. Work until 165 rows are completed.

SHAPE NECKLINE Dec 1 st at end (neck edge) of next and every foll third row at neck edge until 24 sts rem.
At the same time, when chart row 205 is completed, foll chart 2 and work to row 233. Cast off.

SLEEVES

Using 3.25mm needles and col D, cast on 58 sts. Work striped rib as follows:

ROW 1 (RS) *Using col D, k2. Using col A, p2. Rep from * to last 2 sts. Using col D, k2.

JACKET CHART 2: BORDER

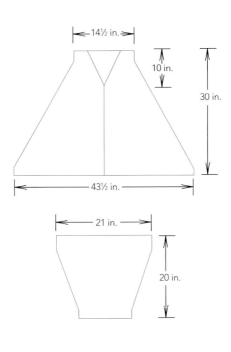

ROW 2 *Using col D, p2. Using col A, k2. Rep from * to last 2 sts. Using col D, p2.
Rep these 2 rows until rib measures 1¼ in. from cast-on edge and ends on a WS row.
Change to 3.75mm needles. Foll chart 3 on pp. 104-105, start with a knit row and work the 158 rows, inc 1 st at both ends of first and every foll fourth row 26 times (110 sts), then every fifth row 8 times (126 sts). Cont to chart row 158, then cast off.

BAND

Join shoulder seams using a small, neat back-stitch on edge of work. Using a 3mm circular needle and col D, start at bottom right front with RS facing. Working back and forth, pick up and knit 126 sts to start of neckline shaping; 52 sts up neckline to shoulder seam; 34 sts across back neck; 52 sts down left front neck edge along neck shaping; and 126 sts down vertical edge to bottom left front (390 sts). Working in moss st, work 8 rows.
At the same time, work buttonholes on row 4: Work 6 sts, (cast off 3 sts, work 20 sts) 3 times, (cast off 3 sts, work 21 sts) twice, cast off 3 sts, work to end.
Cast on these sts when you come to them on next row, working into backs of sts on next row. When 8 rows are completed, knit 1 row to form foldline.
Cont in st st, starting on a knit row, for a further 8 rows, working buttonholes on rows 4 and 5: Work 264 sts, (cast off 3 sts, work 21 sts) twice, (cast off 3 sts, work 20 sts) 3 times, cast off 3 sts, work 6 sts (390 sts). When 8 rows are completed, cast off.

FINISHING

Use a small, neat backstitch on edge of work for seams. Measure 10½ in. down from shoulder seam on both sides of armholes and mark. Find center of sleeves and pin in place at shoulder seam, placing the rest of sleeve at markers. Stitch in place. Join side and sleeve seams in one line from top of rib to top of rib. Join ribs using an invisible edge-to-edge stitch so the ribs will lie flat. Turn band onto WS and slipstitch in place. Sew two sides of buttonholes together around edges. Attach 6 buttons to left front directly opposite buttonholes, making sure that patt is in line.

JACKET CHART 3: SLEEVE

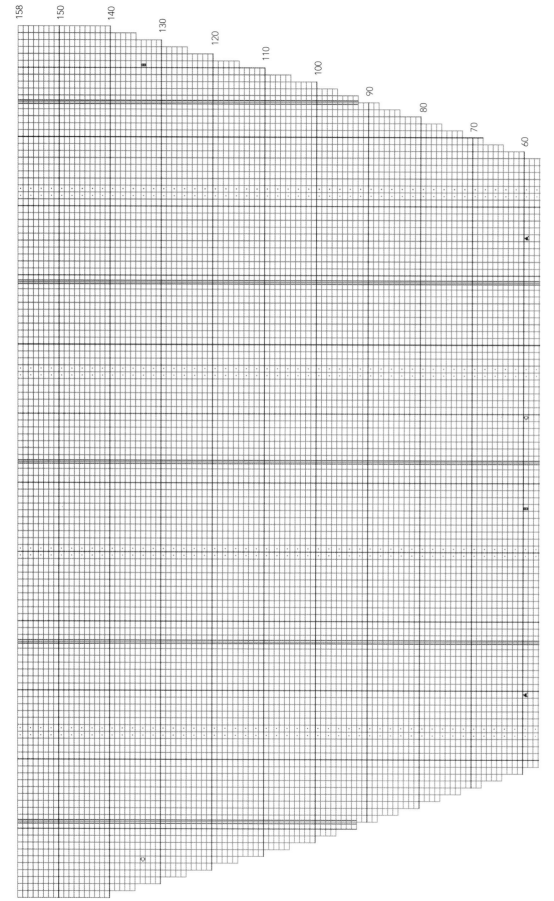

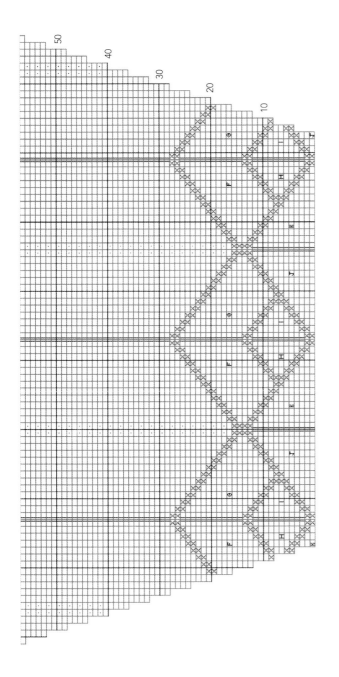

Maya throw in colorway 1 (right)
and colorway 2

T H R O W

NEEDLES
• 5mm (USA 8) circular
• Large crochet hook

TENSION
18 sts and 26 rows = 4 in. or 10cm over patt

MEASUREMENTS
87 in. by 60 in.

YARN
Rowan Magpie Aran

Key		Colorway 1	Colorway 2	Quantity	
⊟	A	Rocket 509	Ember 763	5 hanks	x 100g
	B	Sienna 766	Pumice 301	4 hanks	x 100g
▣	C	Turq 308	Camel 676	4 hanks	x 100g
△	D	Sea Lord 608	Berry 684	6 hanks	x 100g
◇	E	Cork 309	Bordeaux 679	6 hanks	x 100g
☒	F	Spark 767	Sienna 766	2 hanks	x 100g
⊡	G	India 307	India 307	2 hanks	x 100g
⊙	H	Berry 684	Turq 308	1 hank	x 100g
⊞	I	Pesto 768	Pesto 768	1 hank	x 100g
⊘	J	Neptune 612	Sea Lord 608	2 hanks	x 100g
◨	K	Moss 683	Cork 309	2 hanks	x 100g

THROW STITCH KEY
Chart is read from right to left on RS rows and from left to right on WS rows.

☐   rev st st—using background col for that particular stripe, purl on RS and knit on WS

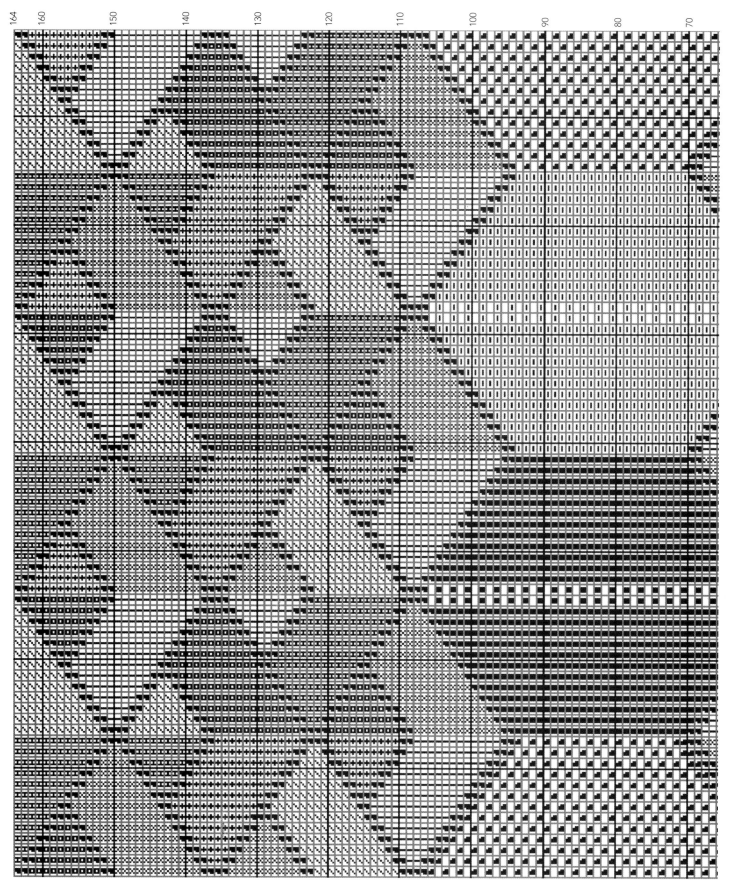

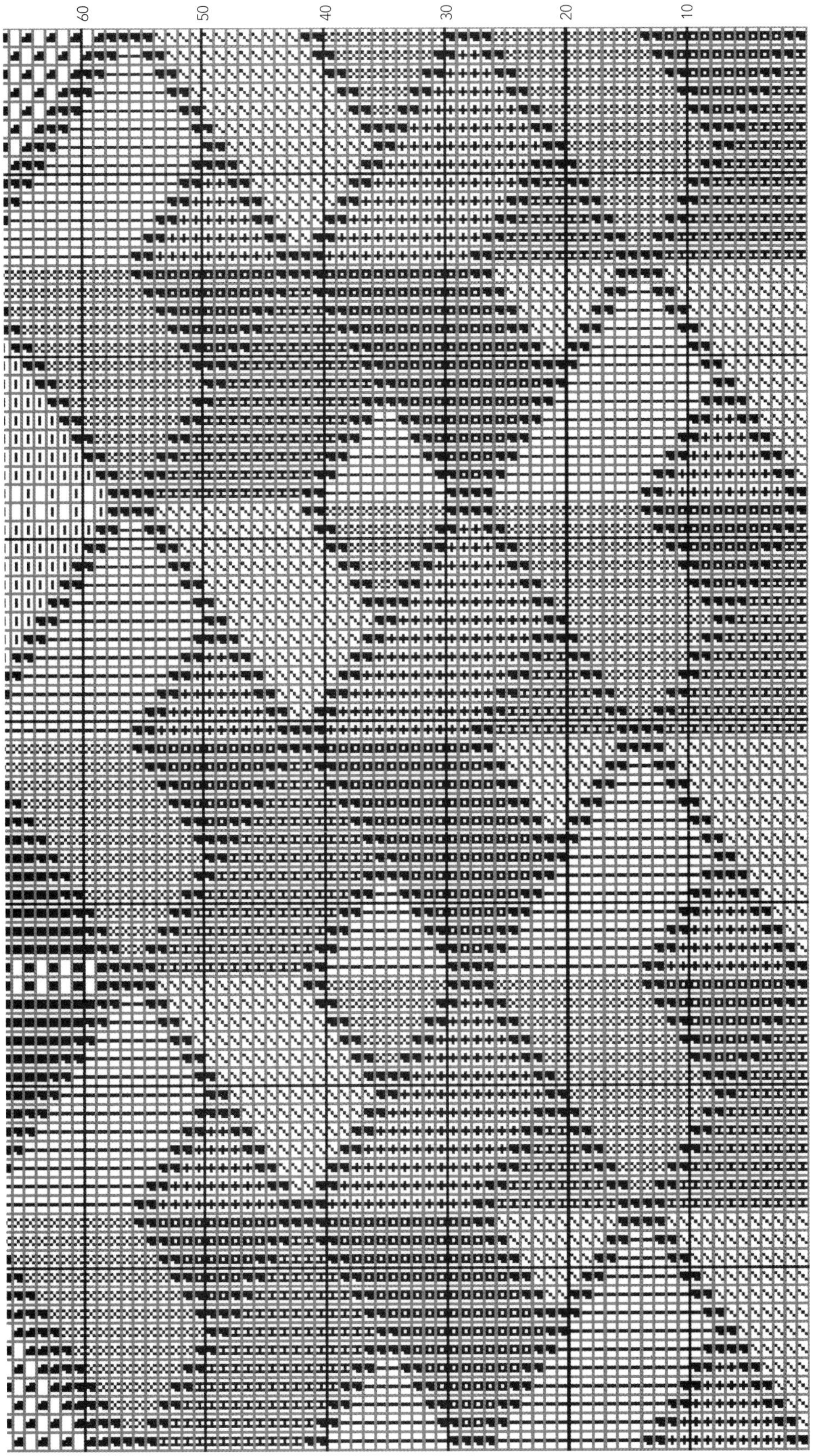
60
50
40
30
20
10

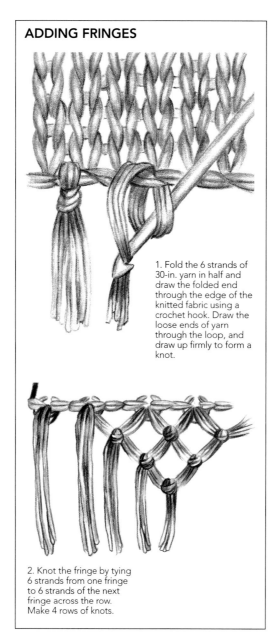

ADDING FRINGES

1. Fold the 6 strands of 30-in. yarn in half and draw the folded end through the edge of the knitted fabric using a crochet hook. Draw the loose ends of yarn through the loop, and draw up firmly to form a knot.

2. Knot the fringe by tying 6 strands from one fringe to 6 strands of the next fringe across the row. Make 4 rows of knots.

KNITTING THE THROW

Using a 5mm circular needle and col D and working back and forth, cast on 284 sts.
Work 7 sts in moss st in col D, then foll the chart on pp. 108-109, work the 78 sts across row 3 times, work the first 26 sts, then work 7 sts in moss st in col D (284 sts).
When 71 rows are completed, foll the col sequence of stripes across blanket:
D A B D C A B D C A D.
Working patt for stripes as set above, rep rows 71 to 94 of chart until work measures 76 in. from cast-on edge. Keeping cols of stripes correct, work rows 93 to 164 of chart. Cast off in col E.

FINISHING

Make a fringed edging along the cast-on and cast-off edges. Make all fringes in col E. Take 6 strands of 30-in. yarn so that when the fringe is on the blanket there are 12 strands of yarn, each measuring approx 14 in. (see the top illustration at left on making the fringes). Using a large crochet hook, insert the fringe from WS to RS so that when pulled through there is a piece of yarn across the top of each fringe. Place the fringes equidistant along the edges, making 4 fringes for every stripe and 2 or 3 fringes for narrower edging stripes. When all fringes are on the blanket, there should be an even number. Make 4 rows of knots by taking 6 strands from one fringe and tying them to 6 strands in the next fringe across the row (leave the first and last 6 strands loose on the first row of knots). Rep this process, starting and ending with the 6 loose strands (see the illustration at left). Rep the first row of knots.

PILLOW

NEEDLES

- 3.75mm (USA 5)
- 4mm (USA 6)
- Large crochet hook

TENSION

28 sts and 28 rows = 4 in. or 10cm over patt

24 sts and 32 rows = 4 in. or 10cm over

moss st

MEASUREMENTS

18½ in. by 18½ in.

FRONT

Using 4mm needles and col D, cast on 132 sts. Foll the chart on pp. 112-113, work the 140 rows, then cast off in col D.

BACK

Using 3.75mm needles and col D, cast on 112 sts. Work in moss st as follows:

ROW 1 *K1, p1, rep from * to end.

ROW 2 *P1, k1, rep from * to end.
These 2 rows form the patt and are rep to end of back. When work measures 18½ in. and ends on a WS row, work 2 rows of purl to form fold-line. **Note:** Make sure that back is same length as front up to here and adjust before working foldline if it is not.
Work a further 3½ in. in moss st, then cast off.

FINISHING

Turn down extra 3½ in. of back onto inside and oversew in place down side seams (do not sew hem across width of pillow). Then with RS facing and using a small, neat backstitch on edge of work, sew around three sides of pillow, leaving top end (with extra 3½ in. turned down) open.

TASSELS

Make 4 tassels, 2 in col A, 2 in col B (see the illustrations on p. 113). Attach the same cols to diagonally opposite corners, with each tassel corresponding to the nearest square of its own col in center design. Take 24 strands of yarn, each 14 in. long, so that when each tassel is on the pillow there are 48 strands that are 6 in. long.

Maya pillow in colorway 1 (front) and colorway 2

YARN
Rowan Designer DK

Key		Colorway 1	Colorway 2	Quantity	
□	A	Lilac 687	Plum 659	1 ball	x 50g
✳	B	Magenta 633	Rust 663	1 ball	x 50g
·	C	Cinnamon 691	Old Gold 690	1 ball	x 50g
△	D	Turquoise 661	Scarlet 632	5 balls	x 50g
⊞	E	Rust 663	Dusty Green 685	1 ball	x 50g
◌	F	Dusty Green 685	Lime 635	1 ball	x 50g
⊟	G	Scarlet 632	Turquoise 661	1 ball	x 50g
⋈	H	Lime 635	Cinnamon 691	1 ball	x 50g
I	I	Old Gold 690	Magenta 633	1 ball	x 50g
⊙	J	Blue 696	Old Rose 070	1 ball	x 50g
⧄	K	Woodland 686	Damson 636	1 ball	x 50g

PILLOW CHART

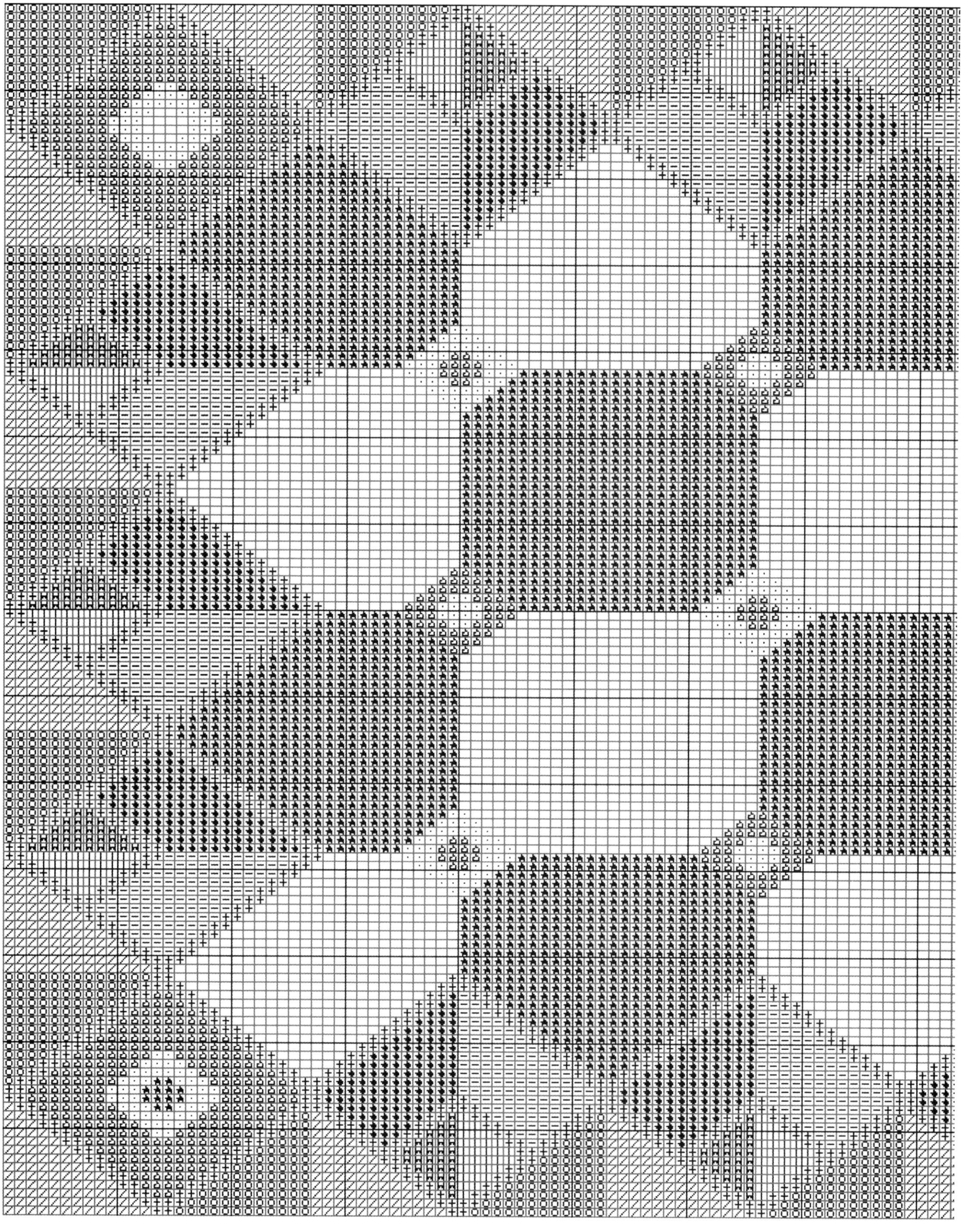

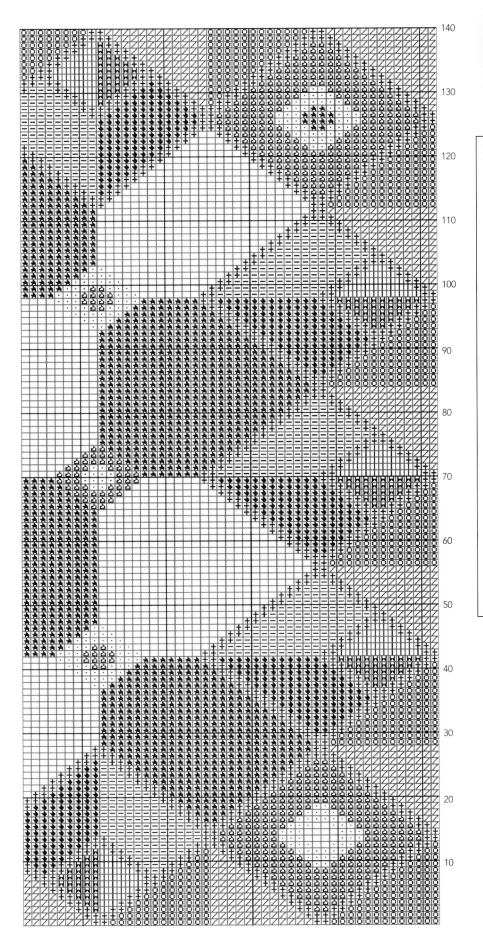

PILLOW STITCH KEY

Chart is read from right to left on RS rows and from left to right on WS rows.

MAKING TASSELS

1. Cut a rectangle of card-board as wide as the required length of the finished tassel. Wind the yarn around the card until the required thickness is reached. Break the yarn, thread through a sewing needle, and pass the needle under all the loops. Do not remove the needle.

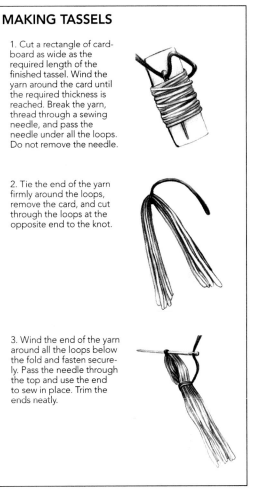

2. Tie the end of the yarn firmly around the loops, remove the card, and cut through the loops at the opposite end to the knot.

3. Wind the end of the yarn around all the loops below the fold and fasten secure-ly. Pass the needle through the top and use the end to sew in place. Trim the ends neatly.

Maya hat

HAT

SIZE
One size

MAKING THE HAT

Make large pieces of felt in each of 4 cols on a knitting machine by casting on 200 sts and working 72 in. per col. (There is no need to cast off in between cols or at the end, as you can cut the fabric without it fraying.) Release the fabric from the knitting machine and cut it into pieces of one col. The pieces must be separated because they will felt together if left in one piece. If you do not have a knitting machine, you can recycle your old sweaters by shrinking them in the washing machine, thereby felting them.

Felt the pieces two at a time in the washing machine at 140°F. Add powdered detergent and an old towel, which provides friction and speeds up the felting process. You may need to put some pieces through twice, but usually wool will felt after only one wash. **Note:** Do not use machine-washable yarn that has been coated with silicone because it will not felt.

Dry the pieces on a radiator or in a dryer.

Cut out 9 pieces in pattern A: 3 pieces in col 1, 3 pieces in col 2, and 3 pieces in col 3. Cut out 1 piece in pattern B in col 4.

Using colorless thread and a straight stitch on a sewing machine, sew the 9 pattern A pieces together down the long sides in the following order: 1 2 3 1 2 3 1 2 3.

Join the first and last pieces to make a circle. Allow ³⁄₁₆ in. for a seam, which will be on the outside (RS) of the hat.

Using zigzag stitch on the sewing machine, sew around the edge of piece B and around the top (larger end) of hat. This will ensure that the fabric does not fray and will give a firmer edge. Pin the crown to the hat and sew in place using straight stitch, making sure that the seams on the stripes are on the outside but the top seam is on the inside.

Choose one of the stripe cols and cut a small circle to handsew onto the middle of the crown using a neat hemming stitch.

Leave the bottom edge unstitched. The fabric will not fray and can be rolled to the desired length.

YARN
Rowan 4-ply Botany knitted on a knitting machine, then felted in a washing machine. Choose 4 cols to match your sweater.

HAT PATTERN A

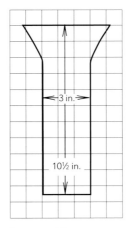

1 square = 1 in.

HAT PATTERN B

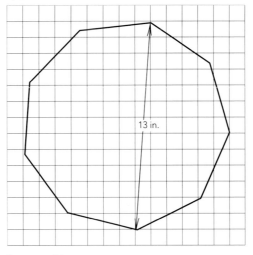

1 square = 1 in.

HAUSA

JACKET

SWEATER

PILLOW

SOCKS

The detail shown above is from a pair of baggy drawstring cotton trousers from Hausaland in northern Nigeria that have an amazing waist measurement of 132 in. Made by men for men, they are traditionally worn beneath long-sleeved, embroidered monochrome robes, which contrast dramatically with the riot of silken trellis-work, knots, loops, diamonds, suns, stripes, and checkerboards of the brilliantly colored trousers. The motifs are highly symbolic and reflect both Islamic and indigenous influences.

I have adopted patterns from these and another pair of trousers that I discovered in the British Museum. What I particularly like about these chaotic designs is their randomness—a fabulously colorful expression of freedom that radiates a feeling of balance and harmony. So in this tradition, the five pieces of the Hausa jacket carry many different symbolic motifs. The border pattern from the hem and cuffs is reduced to a small fairisle design for the shawl collar, interestingly knitted with the fronts in one piece. The jacket is finished with

brilliant brass suns for a chic military look or in square horn buttons carved with geometric lines that echo those in the jacket. The Hausa sweater also uses many of the same ancient symbols, as well as the beautiful sleeve motif, which reminds me of the aurora of the African sunrise. The sweater is completed with checkerboard striped ribs at the welts and collar.

The Hausa socks coordinate perfectly with either the jacket or sweater and are a great practice piece for the two. The Hausa pillow is knitted in chunky chenille for its lusciously extravagant texture and, with its solid-color moss stitch reverse, has the bonus of being a quick knit. The knot motif, used by many different cultures, is a favorite of mine; it symbolizes the interdependence of all the peoples of the world.

The four pieces in this chapter are well within the capabilities of a knitter who enjoys intarsia. I hope that these designs will become a springboard for you to create your own unique collection of Hausa-inspired sweaters and homewares. Experiment and enjoy!

JACKET

NEEDLES

- 3.25mm (USA 3)
- 3.75mm (USA 5)

BUTTONS

Four 30mm brass suns or four 16mm square horn buttons

TENSION

25 sts and 30 rows = 4 in. or 10cm over intarsia patt

SIZE

One size to fit 34-in. to 42-in. bust
See diagram on p. 126 for finished knitted measurements.

YARN

Rowan Cotton Glacé

Key		Colorway 1	Colorway 2	Quantity	
□	A	Black 727	Blood Orange 445	14 balls	x 50g
⁄	B	Dusk 439	Air Force 442	2 balls	x 50g
O	C	Blood Orange 445	Banana 444	2 balls	x 50g
+	D	Parade 430	Black 727	2 balls	x 50g
-	E	Air Force 442	Provence 744	1 ball	x 50g
X	F	Port 245	Damson 226	2 balls	x 50g
△	G	Delft 782	Dusk 439	2 balls	x 50g
V	H	Provence 744	Delft 782	2 balls	x 50g
Z	I	Sunkissed 231	Dijon 739	1 ball	x 50g

Previous page: Hausa sweater (left) and jacket, both in colorway 1

Hausa jacket in colorway 1

BACK

Using 3.25mm needles and col A, cast on 156 sts. Work 15 rows in k1, p1 rib, ending with a RS row.

NEXT ROW (WS) Knit to form foldline for hem. Change to 3.75mm needles. Foll chart 1 on pp. 120-121 until 82 rows are completed.

ARMHOLE SHAPING: ROW 83 (RS) K2, sl 1, k1, psso, work from chart 1 to last 4 sts, k2tog, k2. Work 1 row without shaping. Working all dec in same way as above, dec 1 st at each end of next and every foll alt row 10 times (136 sts). Work without shaping until chart row 153 has been completed and ends with a RS row.

NECK SHAPING: ROW 154 (WS) Work first 52 sts in patt as set, turn, and leave rem sts on a st holder. Working first side of neck only, dec 1 st at beg of next row (neck edge), then at neck edge on foll 3 rows (48 sts). Work 1 row without shaping, then cast off.
Return to rem sts and with WS facing, rejoin yarn and cast off center 32 sts, working in patt as set to end of row. Dec 1 st at end of next row (neck edge), then at neck edge on foll 3 rows (48 sts). Cast off.

LEFT FRONT

POCKET LINING Using 3.75mm needles and col A, cast on 24 sts. Beg with a knit row, work 24 rows in st st, ending with a WS row. Break off yarn and sl sts onto a st holder.

BEGIN FRONT Using 3.25mm needles and col A, cast on 74 sts. Begin k1, p1 rib for hem as follows:

ROW 1 (RS) *P1, k1, rep from * to end.

ROW 2 *P1, k1, rep from * to end.
Rep last 2 rows 6 more times, then rep first row again.

NEXT ROW (WS) Cast on 18 sts and knit to end of row to form foldline for hem (92 sts). Change to 3.75mm needles. Working in st st, foll chart 2 on p. 122 until row 39 has been completed and ends with a RS row.

Hausa jacket in colorway 2 (left) and colorway 1

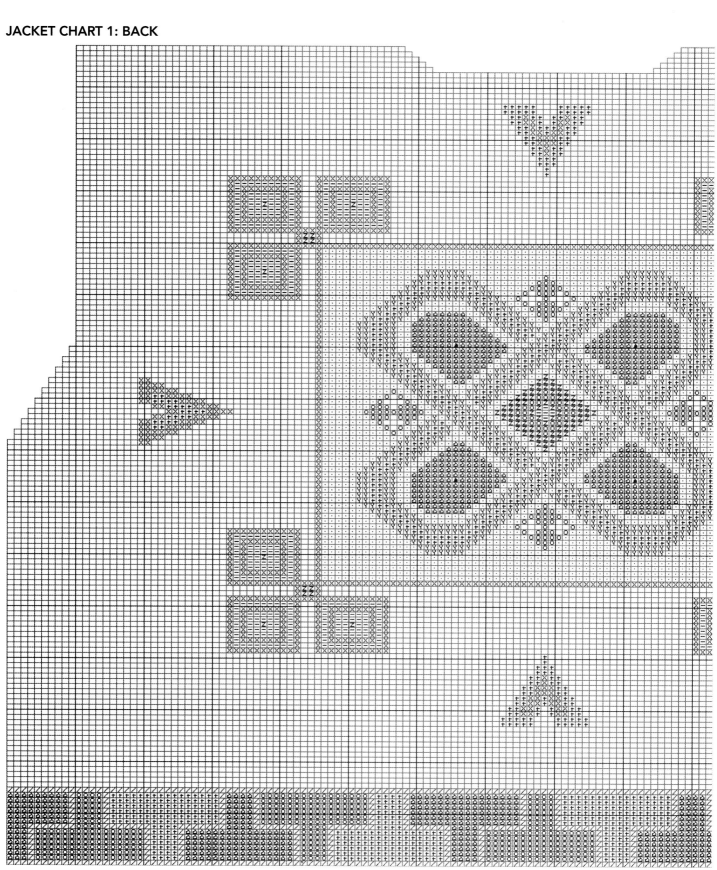

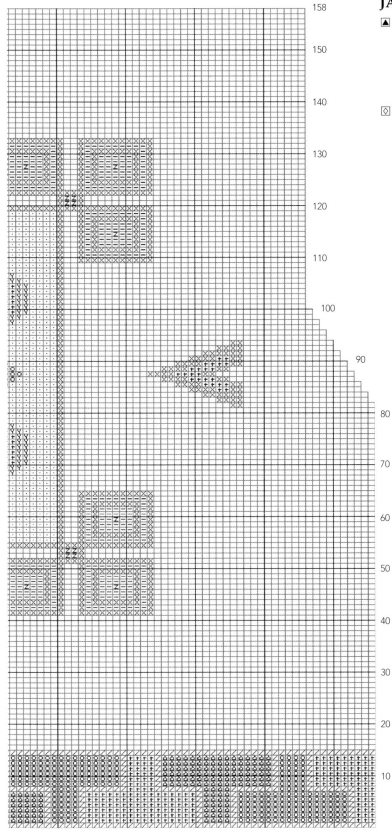

JACKET STITCH KEY

▲   Using col G, knit into this st without slipping it off needle, bring yarn forward, knit again into same st, and sl it off needle. Turn work. Purl the 3 made sts. Turn and knit the 3 made sts. Turn, p2tog, p1. Turn, sl 1, k1, psso. Note: When bobble occurs on WS row, read purl for knit and knit for purl.

◊   Make bobble as above in col A

JACKET CHART 2: LEFT FRONT

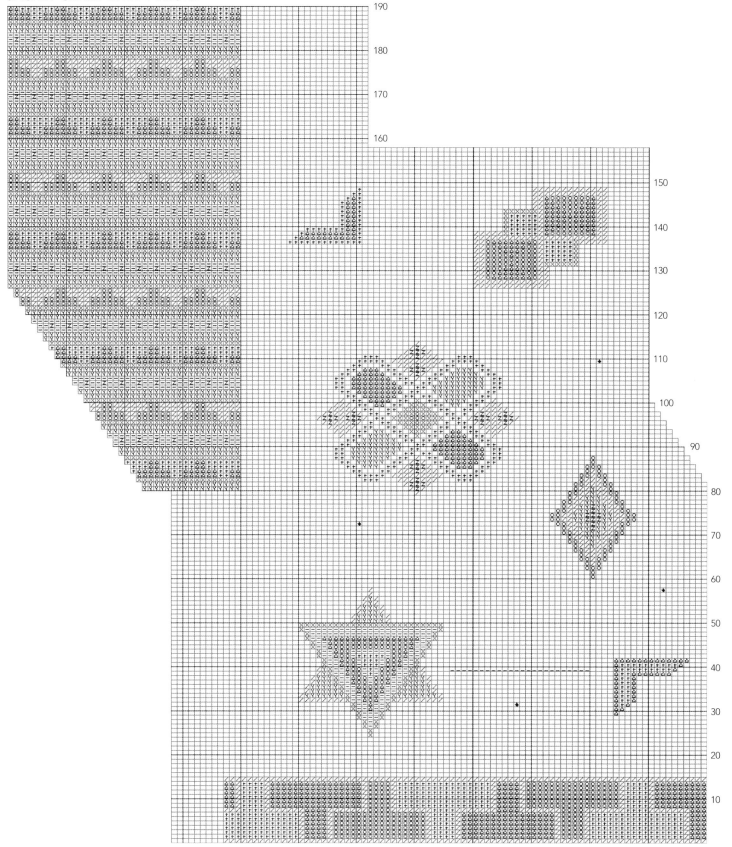

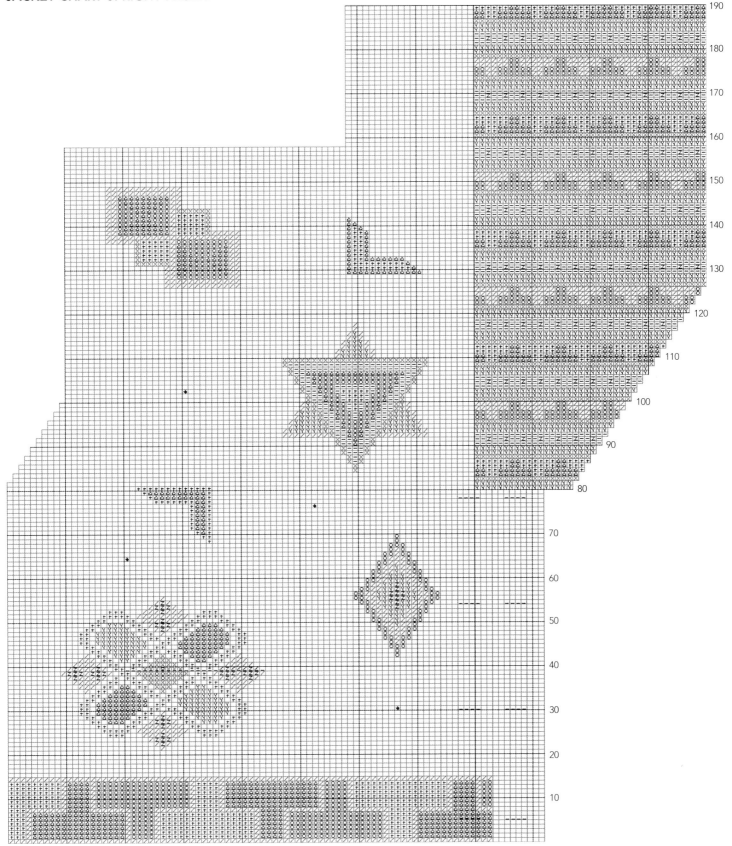

JACKET CHART 4: LEFT SLEEVE

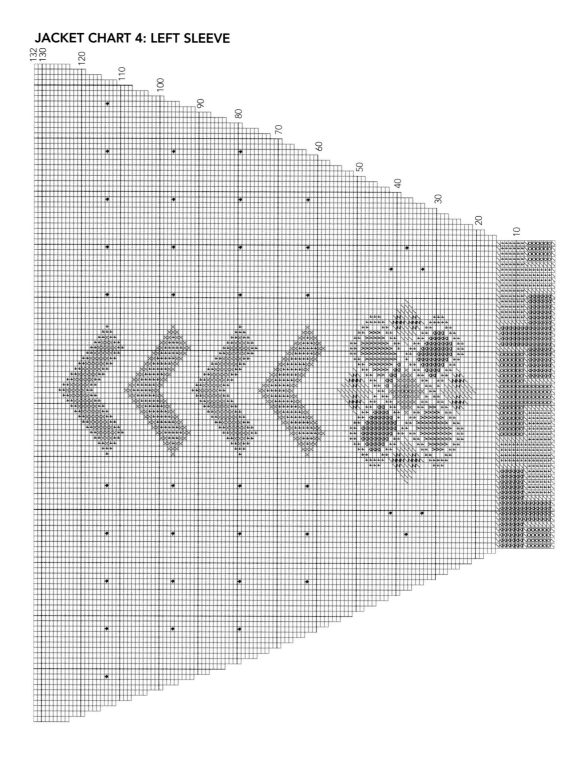

INSERT POCKET LINING: ROW 40 (WS) Work first 48 sts in patt and sl next 24 sts onto a st holder. With WS of pocket lining facing, work in patt across 24 sts of pocket lining, then work rem 20 sts in patt. Work in patt until row 82 has been completed, casting on 5 sts at end of row 81 (97 sts).

ARMHOLE SHAPING Working dec as for back, dec 1 st at beg of chart row 83 (armhole edge), then at armhole edge on every foll alt row 10 times.

At the same time, inc 1 st at neck edge on chart row 83, then every alt row 23 times (110 sts). Work without shaping until chart row 158 is completed and ends with a WS row.

SHOULDER SHAPING: ROW 159 (RS) Cast off 48 sts and work in patt to end.

COLLAR EXTENSION Work collar extension without shaping on rem 62 sts until chart row 190 has been completed and ends with a WS row. Cast off.

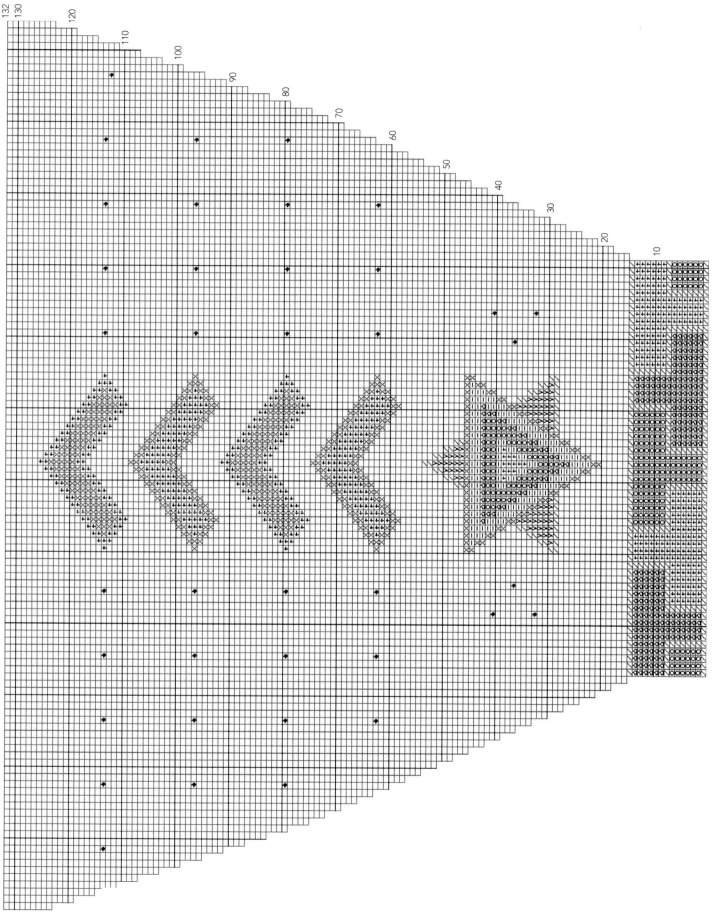

RIGHT FRONT

Work as for left front, but foll chart 3 on p. 123, rev all shapings and position of pockets. Work buttonholes on rows indicated. For 4 double buttonholes, cast off 4 sts as per chart and cast on these sts on foll row when you come to them. Work into backs of these sts on foll row.

LEFT SLEEVE

Using 3.25mm needles and col A, cast on 58 sts. Work 15 rows in k1, p1 rib, ending with a RS row.

NEXT ROW (WS)   Knit to form foldline for hem. Change to 3.75mm needles. Working in st st, foll chart 4 on p. 124 until row 15 has been completed and ends with a RS row. Cont to foll chart for patt, inc 1 st at each end of next and every foll third row until there are 100 sts, then every fourth row until there are 124 sts (row 124). Cont to foll chart without shaping until row 132 has been completed. Cast off.

RIGHT SLEEVE

Work as for left sleeve but foll chart 5 on p. 125 for patt.

FINISHING

Press pieces lightly on WS with a warm iron over a damp cloth, omitting ribs.

POCKET HEMS   With RS facing and using 3.25mm needles and col A, knit across 24 sts of left front pocket and knit 1 row to form hemline fold. Work 6 rows in k1, p1 rib, then cast off. Work hem at top of other pocket in same way. Turn pocket hems to WS and slipstitch in place. Slipstitch pocket linings to WS of fronts.
Use a small, neat backstitch on edge of work for all seams except ribs, where an invisible slipstitch should be used so the ribs will lie flat. Join shoulder seams. Find center of sleeves and mark. Place center of top of sleeve at shoulder seam, then sew cast-off edge of sleeves to armhole edge (including dec edge). Join side and sleeve seams in one line.
Turn hem on back and fronts to WS along purl row above ribbing and slipstitch in place.
Turn hem on sleeves to WS in same way and slipstitch in place.
Join cast-off edges of collar extension. Sew collar extension to back neck, easing in collar. Fold collar in half (WS together) and fold front button and buttonhole band facings to WS (9 sts from edge) and slipstitch in place. Sew two layers of each buttonhole together around edge. Sew buttons to button band to correspond with buttonholes.

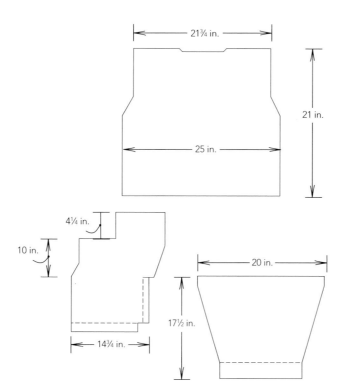

SWEATER

NEEDLES
- 4mm (USA 6)
- 5mm (USA 8)
- 4mm (USA 6) circular

TENSION
18 sts and 26 rows = 4 in. or 10cm over patt

SIZE
One size to fit 34-in. to 44-in. bust
See diagram on p. 131 for finished knitted measurements.

YARN
Rowan Magpie Aran

Key		Colorway 1	Colorway 2	Quantity	
☐	A	Comanche 503	Sea Lord 608	9 hanks	x 100g
⊟	B	Ember 763	Neptune 612	1 hank	x 100g
☑ Z	C	Bordeaux 679	Moss 683	1 hank	x 100g
⊘ /	D	Sea Lord 608	Comanche 503	1 hank	x 100g
⊞ E	E	Neptune 612	Damson 511	1 hank	x 100g
△ F	F	Pumice 301	Ocean 305	1 hank	x 100g
⊙ G	G	Ginger 505	Rocket 509	1 hank	x 100g
☒ H	H	Woodland 300	Ginger 505	1 hank	x 100g
☑ V	I	Ocean 305	Thunder 764	1 hank	x 100g

Hausa sweater in colorway 1

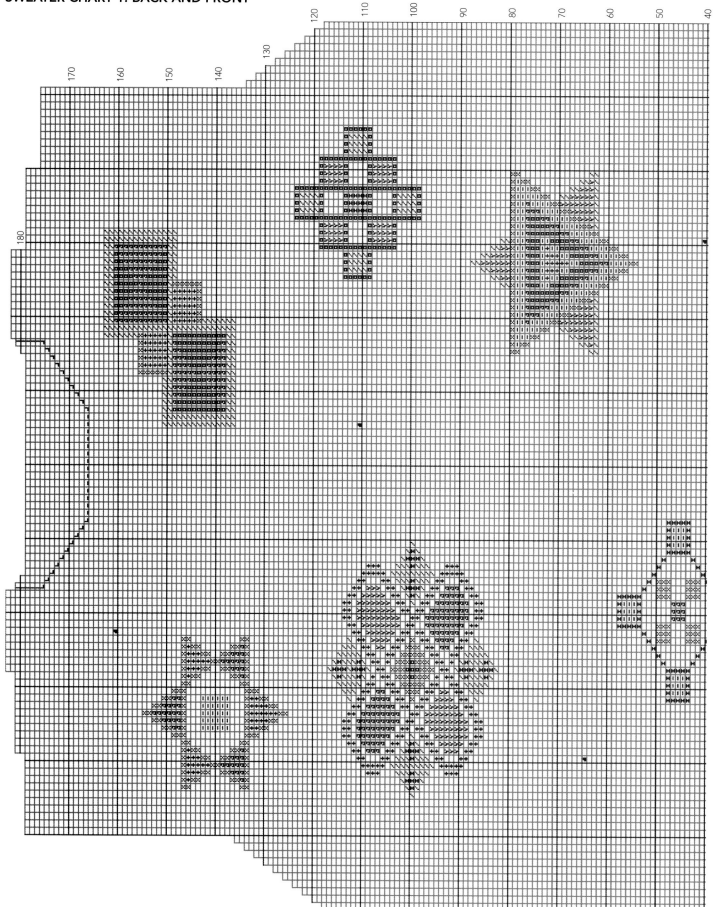

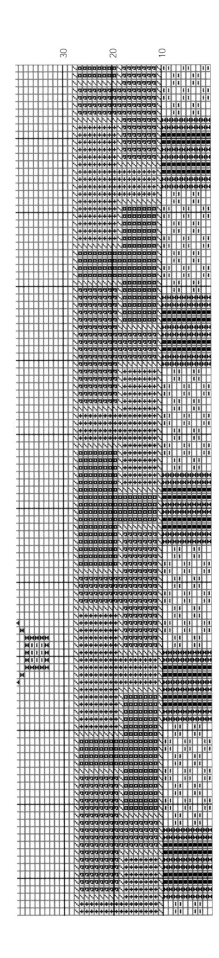

BACK

Using col A and 4mm needles, cast on 120 sts. Foll chart 1 at left, work first 10 rows. Change to 5mm needles and cont to work from chart until row 118 is completed.

SHAPE ARMHOLES: ROW 119 K2, sl 1, k1, psso, work to last 4 sts, k2tog, k2.
Dec as above every alt row 9 times (102 sts).
Cont from chart until row 178 is completed.

SHAPE SHOULDER AND NECKLINE Cast off 11 sts at beg of next row. Cast off 11 sts at beg of next row, work 25 sts, and place rem 55 sts on a st holder. Turn and dec 1 st at beg (neck edge) of next row, work to end. Cast off 11 sts at beg of next row, work to last 2 sts, p2tog. Work 1 row, then cast off rem 12 sts.
Leaving 30 sts at center back on a st holder, rejoin yarn at neck edge and work 1 row. Cast off 11 sts at beg of next row, work to last 2 sts, k2tog. Dec 1 st at beg of next row, work to end. Cast off rem 12 sts.

FRONT

Work as for back until row 166 is completed.

SHAPE NECKLINE Work the first 43 sts, turn, and leave rem 59 sts on a st holder. Dec 1 st at neck edge on next and every row 9 times (34 sts). Cont foll chart until row 178 is completed.

SHAPE SHOULDER Cast off 11 sts at beg of next row. Work 1 row. Cast off 11 sts at beg of next row. Work 1 row. Cast off rem 12 sts. Leave 16 sts at center front on a st holder and rejoin yarn at other side of neck edge.
Work 1 row, then dec 1 st at neck edge on next and foll 8 rows until there are 34 sts. Cont foll chart until row 179 is completed.

SWEATER STITCH KEY

◼   rev st st—using col A, purl on RS and knit on WS
◇   make small bobble in col A—knit into this st without slipping it off needle, bring yarn forward, knit again into same st and sl it off needle. Turn work. Purl the 3 made sts. Turn and knit the 3 made sts. Turn, p2tog, p1. Turn, sl 1, k1, psso.

SWEATER CHART 2: SLEEVE

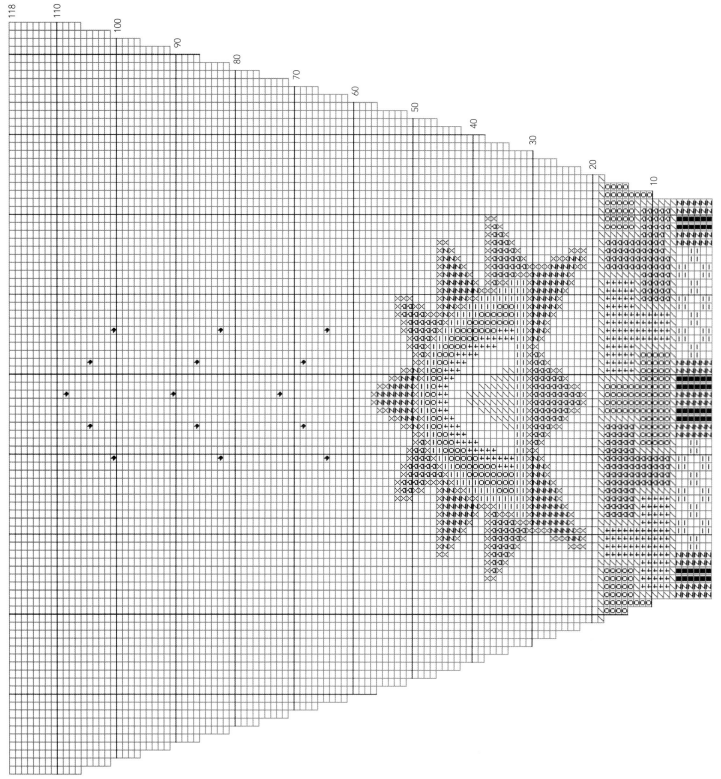

SHAPE SHOULDER Cast off 11 sts at beg of next row. Work 1 row. Cast off 11 sts at beg of next row. Work 1 row. Cast off rem 12 sts.

SLEEVES

Using col A and 4mm needles, cast on 50 sts. Foll chart 2 on the facing page, work first 6 rows. Change to 5mm needles and cont with chart, inc 1 st at both ends of row 11, then every fourth row 9 times (70 sts) and every fifth row 12 times (94 sts). Cont until row 118 is completed, then cast off.

NECKBAND

Join right shoulder seam using a small, neat backstitch on edge of work, just inside cast-off edges so that cast-off edge does not show on RS.

Using a circular 4mm needle and col A, start at left shoulder with RS facing. Pick up and knit 5 sts down straight edge of front neck; 14 sts down sloping front neck edge; 16 sts from st holder at center front; 14 sts up sloping neck edge; 5 sts up straight front neck edge to right shoulder; 3 sts down back neck edge; 30 sts from st holder at center back; and 3 sts up back neck edge (90 sts).

Foll chart 3 at right and working back and forth, rep the 18 sts 5 times across every row. Work 16 rows, then cast off in col A.

FINISHING

Use a small, neat backstitch on edge of work for all seams except ribs, where an invisible slipstitch should be used so the ribs will lie flat. Join left shoulder seam and neckband. Insert sleeves, placing straight edge of sleeve along armhole edge. Join side and sleeve seams in one line.

SWEATER CHART 3: NECKBAND

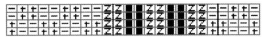

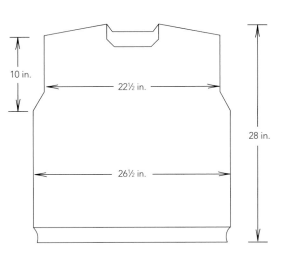

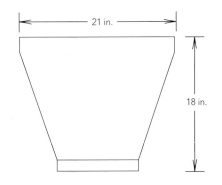

Hausa pillow in colorway 1 (front) and colorway 2

PILLOW

NEEDLES
• 5.5mm (USA 9)
• 6mm (USA 10)
• 6mm (USA 10) crochet hook

TENSION
14 sts and 22 rows = 4 in. over intarsia patt and over moss st

MEASUREMENTS
20 in. by 15 in.

YARN
Rowan Chunky Cotton Chenille (cols A, B in colorway 2, D in colorway 1, E, F, G); Rowan Magpie Aran (cols B in colorway 1, C, D in colorway 2)

Key		Colorway 1	Colorway 2	Quantity	
⊡	A	Elephant 348	Aubergine 356	2 balls	x 100g
Ⅴ	B	Sienna 766		1 hank	x 100g
			Claret 376	1 ball	x 100g
⊞	C	Ember 763	Elephant 348	1 hank	x 100g
⊙	D	Fern 364		1 ball	x 100g
			Comanche 503	1 hank	x 100g
⊘	E	French Mustard 363	Serge 378	1 ball	x 100g
△	F	Forest Green 362	French Mustard 363	2 balls	x 100g
⊠	G	Serge 378	Forest Green 362	1 ball	x 100g

BACK
Using 5.5mm needles and col F, cast on 71 sts. Work 87 rows in moss st as follows: *k1, p1, rep from * to end. This row forms the patt and is repeated to end of work. When 87 rows are completed, cast off.

FRONT
Using 6mm needles and col A, cast on 71 sts. Foll the chart on the facing page, work the 87 rows. Purl 2 rows to mark foldline for hem. Work a further 3½ in. in col A in st st, then cast off.

FINISHING
Use a small, neat backstitch on edge of work for all seams. Turn down an extra 3½ in. of front on inside and oversew in place down sideseams (do not sew the hem across width of pillow). Using a crochet hook and col E and with WS of pillow facing (RS on outside), work 1 row of double crochet through back and front at same time around three sides. Leave the top end with the extra 3½ in. open, but cont to crochet along single front edge on mark made by 2 rows of purl. When starting point is reached, fasten off securely on inside.

PILLOW CHART

87
80
70
60
50
40
30
20
10

PILLOW STITCH KEY

▲   rev st st—using col F, purl on RS and knit on WS

Hausa socks in colorway 2 (left) and colorway 1

SOCKS

NEEDLES

- Set of four double-pointed 3.75mm (USA 5)
- Tapestry needle

TENSION

24 sts and 30 rows = 4 in. or 10cm over st st

SIZE

To fit U.S. shoe sizes 5½ to 8½ (English sizes 4 to 7)

LEG

Cast on 48 sts with col F over the index finger and col E over the thumb using the continental method (see p. 8). Make a loop using both cols (loop does not figure in the total st count). When all sts have been cast on, remove the loop made up of the two cols. Divide the sts evenly onto 3 needles. Join into a rnd, being careful not to twist sts. This join marks the seam-line and beg of the rnd.

YARN

Rowan Lightweight DK

Key		Colorway 1	Colorway 2	Quantity	
◆	A	Blue 54	Black 062	1 hank	x 25g
⧄	B	Gold 9	Red 45	1 hank	x 25g
⊡	C	Red 45	Green 91	2 hanks	x 25g
◣	D	Brown 107	Blue 53	1 hank	x 25g
⊞	E	Black 062	Wine 132	1 hank	x 25g
⊠	F	Aqua 100	Gold 9	1 hank	x 25g
✳	G	Wine 132	DK Burgundy 659	1 hank	x 25g

BRAID PATTERN: RND 1 *K1 col F, k1 col E, rep from * around.

RND 2 Bring both cols to front of work, keeping them in the same order as on previous rnd. *P1 col F, p1 col E, always bringing the next col to be used *over* the top of the last col used. Rep from * around.

RND 3 *P1 col F, p1 col E, always bringing the next col to be used *under* the last col used. Rep from * around.
Rep these 3 rnds one more time.
Foll chart 1 on the facing page, work the 19 rows, reading from right to left on all rows since all are knit rows. Foll chart 2 on the facing page, work the 30 rows down to toe, rep the 8 sts 6 times across row.

DIVIDE FOR HEEL Place the first 12 sts and the last 12 sts of the rnd onto one needle for the heel. Place the rem 24 sts onto another needle for the instep.

ROW 1 With RS facing, join col B (working over the 24 sts for heel, *not* the instep sts). Working back and forth on these sts only, *k1, sl 1, rep from * across row.

ROW 2 Purl.
Rep these 2 rows for 2 in., ending on RS.

TURN HEEL Using col B, p14, p2tog, p1, turn work, sl the first st, k5, k2tog, k1. *Turn, sl the first st, purl over to within 1 st of the hole made by slipping the st, purl the 2 sts on either side of the hole together, p1. Rep from *, always slipping the first st, then knitting or purling the 2 together on each side of the hole until all sts are used up (14 sts rem on needle 1).

GUSSET

Using col E and needle 1, pick up and k12 sts along right side of heel. With needle 2, work across the 24 sts of the instep. With needle 3, pick up and k12 sts along left side of heel, and with the same needle k7 sts from needle 1. You should now have 19 sts on needle 1, 24 sts on needle 2, and 19 sts on needle 3. Work 1 rnd, keeping chart 2 correct across row.

SOCKS CHART 1

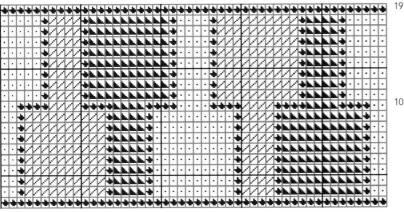

19

10

SOCKS CHART 2

30

20

10

NEXT AND EVERY ALT RND   Dec 1 st at the *front* ends of needles 1 and 3 (the ends of the back needles nearest the front instep needle) by knitting together the second and third sts from the ends. Cont dec 7 times in all (14 rows knitted). You will then have 12 sts each on needles 1 and 3 and 24 sts on needle 2. Keep chart 2 correct while doing the above by working chart 2 as follows:

Work the last 4 sts, work the 8 sts, work the first 7 sts, work the last 4 sts, work the 8 sts twice, work the first 4 sts, work the last 7 sts, work the 8 sts, work the first 4 sts. As you dec 7 times, gradually the first and last 7 sts will dec to 6, 5, 4, etc., so after 14 rows, work the last 4 sts, work the 8 sts 5 times, work the first 4 sts.

FOOT

Cont to foll chart 2 until sock measures 6 in. from beg of gusset. This should be up to row 16 of chart 2 (45 rows in all) but correct here for length if row gauge is off.

Note: Make sure that if you end on the fairisle part that you complete those 4 rows of patt.

SHAPE TOE   Using col C, dec 4 times in a rnd as follows:

Knit to 3 sts from end of needle 1, k2tog, k1. K1, ssk, work to 3 sts from end of needle 2, k2tog, k1. K1, ssk at beg of needle 3, knit to end. Knit 4 rnds plain. Dec in the next rnd as before. Knit 3 rnds plain. Dec in the next rnd. Knit 2 rnds plain. Dec in the next rnd. Knit 1 rnd plain. Dec in the next rnd. Knit 1 rnd plain. Dec in the next 4 rnds. You will have 6 sts on needle 2 and 3 sts each on needles 1 and 3.

FINISHING

Weave the rem sts together using Kitchener stitch (see p. 9) as follows: You should have 6 sts on needle 2. The 3 sts each on needles 1 and 3 should be on one needle, so sl them or knit them so that the yarn is at the end of the needle. Hold the two needles parallel and close together with the yarn coming from the RH end of the back needle. Break the yarn, leaving a 10-in. end. Thread it onto a tapestry needle. Work in Kitchener stitch. Weave in end and snip off.

B A N J A R A

SWEATER

JACKET

HAT

The great wanderers of India, the Banjara gypsies make textiles that are instantly recognizable. Variously adorned with mirrorwork *(shisha)*, sequins, coins, buttons, beads, and cowrie shells, the textiles are extravagantly colorful, intricately embroidered masterpieces of needlework. The girl's skirt from Deccan shown above is finished at the hem and waist with typical *shisha* embroidery, which is believed by the Banjara to trap, dazzle, or even blind the evil eye.

The Banjara sweater is a near-literal interpretation of the skirt's stripes, coupled with some other ideas from a Banjara child's jacket, which I jotted down in a notebook some years ago. The blocks of color are surprisingly easy to work, and I've been told by many knitters that these bright colors have an uplifting effect, forever making you want to knit just one more row! Once the sweater is knitted, you have a canvas on which to create your own personal fantasy. You can add as much or

as little decoration as you wish. Whether you choose to be wildly abandoned or tastefully restrained, you can be sure that you will be noticed wearing this sweater.

In the Banjara jacket, I have developed the small diamonds that are the building blocks of the striped motifs in the sweater. Knitted in kid silk, the jacket is decorated with glass beads. You can knit in the sculptured knot at the center of every diamond or add the bobbles afterward, making the jacket a solid-color knit. Finished with a decorative clasp, the jacket would also look wonderful fastened with your favorite pin.

As I'm definitely a hat person, I couldn't resist including the outrageous Banjara hat. It can be a lengthy project for winter evenings by the fire if you choose to embroider and embellish it, but a quicker alternative is to decorate the hat with a felted posy of three roses (as for the Albion hat) or to use offcuts of felt to appliqué a bold, geometric design around the brim.

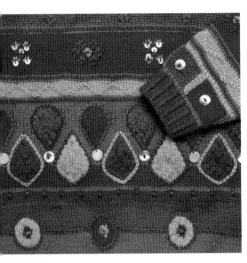

SWEATER

NEEDLES

- 3.25mm (USA 3)
- 3.75mm (USA 5)
- Four double-pointed or circular 3mm (USA 2)

BUTTONS

Decorate to personal taste with sequins, buttons, and beads

TENSION

24 sts and 32 rows = 4 in. or 10cm over patt

SIZE

One size to fit 34-in. to 44-in. bust
See diagram on p. 143 for finished knitted measurements.

YARN

Rowan Lightweight DK

Key		Colorway 1	Colorway 2	Quantity	
☐	A	Red 45	Teal 91	9 hanks	x 25g
◯	B	Brown 604	Dark Blue 54	6 hanks	x 25g
☒	C	Gold 9	Gold 9	5 hanks	x 25g
☑	D	Teal 91	Red 45	4 hanks	x 25g
⊞	E	Rust 77	Rust 77	5 hanks	x 25g
⊘	F	Dark Blue 54	Brown 604	4 hanks	x 25g

Previous page: Banjara short-version jacket (left) and sweater in colorway 1

BACK

Using 3.25mm needles and col E, cast on 156 sts. Work in striped rib as follows:

ROW 1   *K2 col E, p2 col F, rep from * to end.

ROW 2   *K2 col F, p2 col E, rep from * to end.
Rep these 2 rows until work measures 2 in. and ends with a WS row.
Change to 3.75mm needles. Foll chart 1 on pp. 140-141, beg working the 185 rows.

SHAPE ARMHOLE   When row 100 is completed, cast off 12 sts at beg of next 2 rows. Cont in patt as set on chart until row 172 is completed.

SHAPE NECK   Work 51 sts, turn, and leave rem 81 sts on a st holder. Dec 1 st at beg of next row (neck edge) and then at neck edge on every subsequent row 7 times (44 sts). Cont as set to row 181.

SHAPE SHOULDER: ROW 181   Cast off 14 sts at beg of row.

ROW 182   Work across all sts.

ROW 183   Cast off 15 sts at beg of row.

ROW 184   Work across all sts.

ROW 185   Cast off rem 15 sts.
Leave center 30 sts on a st holder, rejoin yarn to rem 51 sts, and work to end. Dec 1 st at end of next (neck edge) and every subsequent row 7 times. Cast off sts for shoulder on rows 182, 184, and 186.

FRONT

Work as for back, but commence neck shaping on chart row 169, leaving center front sts on a st holder.

SLEEVES

Using 3.25mm needles and col E, cast on 52 sts. Work 1½ in. in striped rib as on back and front, ending with a WS row.
Change to 3.75mm needles. Foll chart 2 on pp. 142-143, work the 138 rows, inc 1 st at both ends of every third row 14 times (80 sts), then every fourth row 20 times (120 sts). Cont to work from chart until row 138 is completed, then cast off.

Banjara sweater in colorway 1

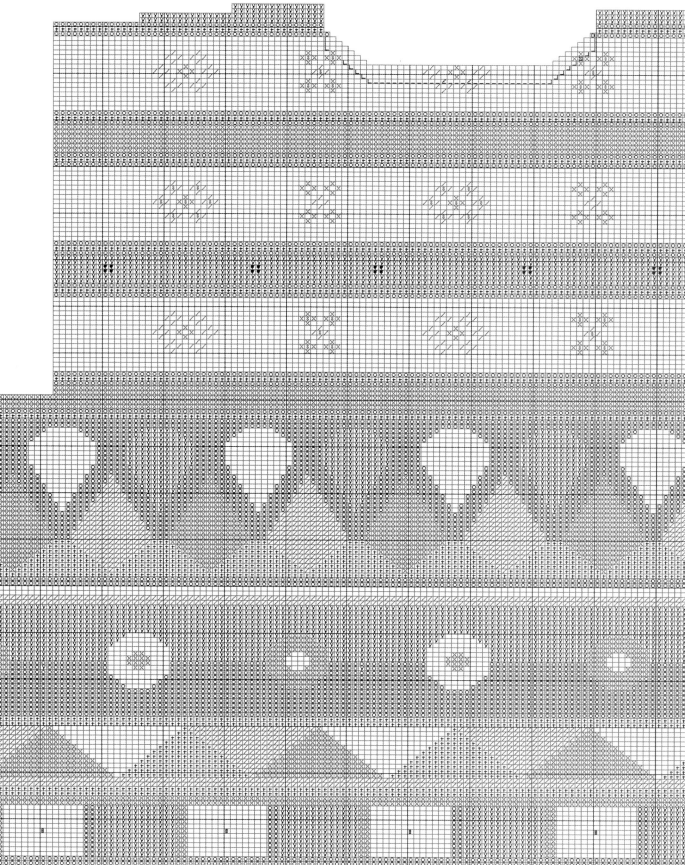

SWEATER STITCH KEY

B	attach button here
S	attach sequin here
▼	use eye st to make star in col D

CHAINSTITCH

Starting with a tapestry needle on RS of work, put the needle back through the same hole, thus making a loop the size of the stitch required, then bring the needle back to RS through the loop to secure it.

EYE STITCH

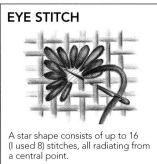

A star shape consists of up to 16 (I used 8) stitches, all radiating from a central point.

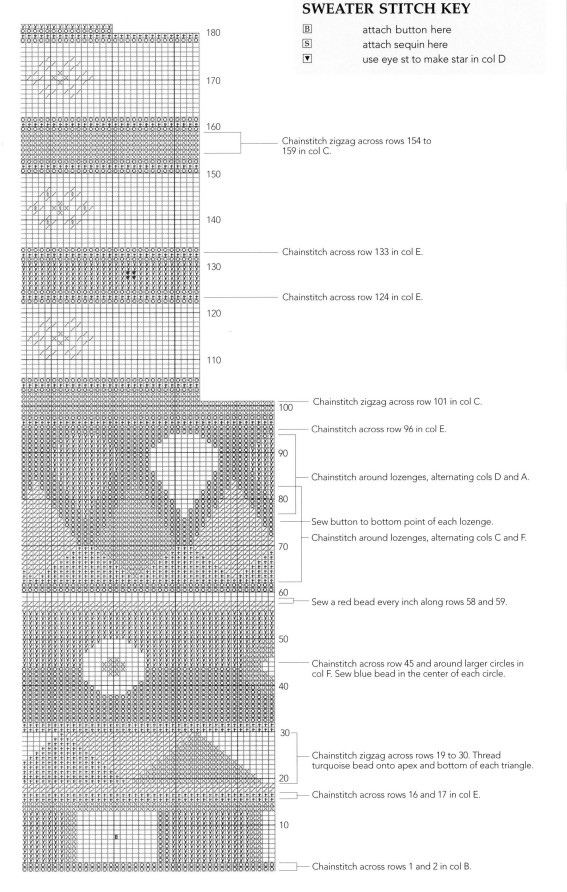

180

170

160 — Chainstitch zigzag across rows 154 to 159 in col C.

150

140

130 — Chainstitch across row 133 in col E.

120 — Chainstitch across row 124 in col E.

110

100 — Chainstitch zigzag across row 101 in col C.

— Chainstitch across row 96 in col E.

90

— Chainstitch around lozenges, alternating cols D and A.

80

— Sew button to bottom point of each lozenge.
— Chainstitch around lozenges, alternating cols C and F.

70

60 — Sew a red bead every inch along rows 58 and 59.

50

— Chainstitch across row 45 and around larger circles in col F. Sew blue bead in the center of each circle.

40

30 — Chainstitch zigzag across rows 19 to 30. Thread turquoise bead onto apex and bottom of each triangle.

20

— Chainstitch across rows 16 and 17 in col E.

10

— Chainstitch across rows 1 and 2 in col B.

SWEATER CHART 2: SLEEVES

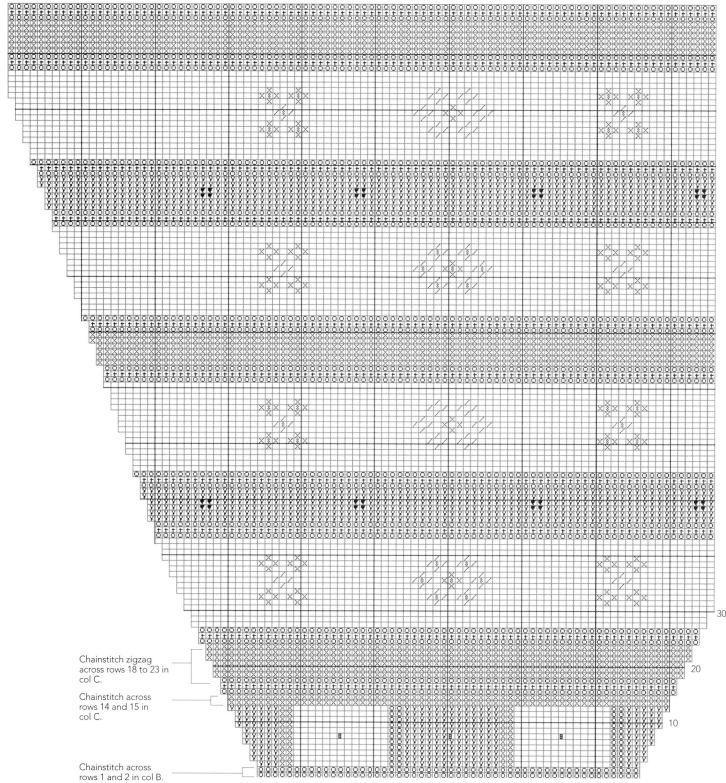

Chainstitch zigzag across rows 18 to 23 in col C.

Chainstitch across rows 14 and 15 in col C.

Chainstitch across rows 1 and 2 in col B.

30

20

10

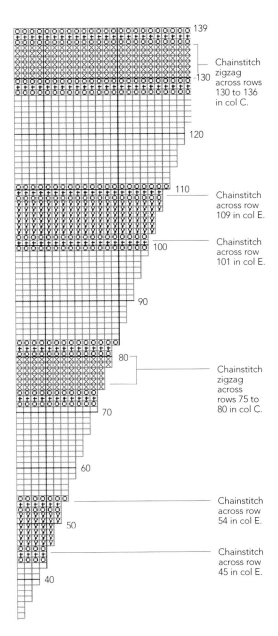

139

Chainstitch zigzag across rows 130 to 136 in col C.

130

120

110

Chainstitch across row 109 in col E.

100

Chainstitch across row 101 in col E.

90

80

Chainstitch zigzag across rows 75 to 80 in col C.

70

60

Chainstitch across row 54 in col E.

50

Chainstitch across row 45 in col E.

40

NECKBAND

Join shoulder seams using a small, neat back-stitch on very edge of work, making sure that the cast-off edge does not show on RS.
Using 4 double-pointed or circular 3mm needles and col E, start at left shoulder seam with RS facing. Pick up and knit 8 sts down front neck edge; 12 sts along sloping front neck edge; 30 sts from st holder at center front; 12 sts up other side sloping neck edge; 8 sts up to shoulder seam; 4 sts down back neck edge; 14 sts along sloping back neck edge; 30 sts from st holder at center back; 14 sts up sloping neck edge; and 4 sts along vertical neck edge to shoulder (136 sts).
Work 2¾ in. in striped rib (all rows RS) as follows: *k2 col E, p2 col F, rep from * around.
Cast off in rib in col E.

FINISHING

Use a small, neat backstitch on very edge of work for all seams and an invisible slipstitch for ribs so they will lie flat. Insert sleeves by placing the cast-off edge of sleeve along vertical arm-hole edge. Sew the top 2 in. of sleeve along horizontal armhole edge. Join side and sleeve seams in one line. Work embroidery where indicated on charts. Sew on buttons, beads, and sequins where indicated on charts or use personal preference and improvise.

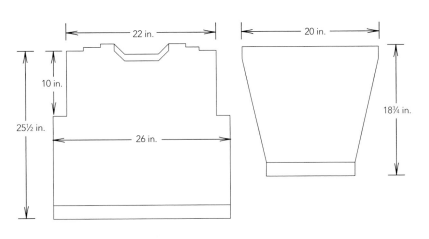

YARN

Rowan Kid Silk (col A); Rowan Lurex (col B)

Key		Short version	Long version	Quantity	
☐	A	Steel Blue 991		20 hanks	x 25g
			Goat Brown 994	24 hanks	x 25g
⊡	B	Silver Lurex 841	Gold Lurex 842	1 hank	x 25g

JACKET

NEEDLES
- 3mm (USA 2)
- 3.75mm (USA 5)

BEADS
250g of knitters' beads: silver for long version, gold for short version

FASTENER
1 frog fastener or clasp

TENSION
24 sts and 30 rows = 4 in. over st st

SIZE
One size to fit 32-in. to 40-in. bust
See diagram on p. 148 for finished knitted measurements.

BEADING
When starting a ball of yarn, thread the required number of beads onto the yarn using a needle, then bring up into position on RS when required. **Note:** The plain st st at the bottom of the jacket will tell you how many rows one ball will knit, and hence, using the chart, how many beads to thread.

LUREX COLORS
The lurex colors are knitted as a small bobble on the RS of work: (k1, p1) twice in the st. Pull up sts loosely, then pass the first, second, and third sts, *in this order*, over the fourth st. Use a separate length of lurex yarn for each bobble. When the bobble is completed, knot the two ends together and run them into the back of the bobble or along the WS of the work.

MOSS STITCH
Knitted over an odd number of sts—k1, p1 to end on every row.
Knitted over an even number of sts—
Row 1 *k1, p1, rep from * to end.
Row 2 *p1, k1, rep from * to end. Rep these 2 rows. Sl the first st and knit into the back of the last st on every row.

Banjara long-version jacket

BACK

Note: Figures in brackets refer to longer version. Using 3mm needles and col A, cast on 140 sts. Work 16 rows in moss st. Change to 3.75mm needles and work straight in st st until work measures 9½ in. [20½ in.] from cast-on edge, ending with a WS row.

Foll chart below, work the 72 rows in st st, introducing the beads on the RS where indicated by Xs.

Work the dec for armhole shaping as follows: k2, sl 1, k1, psso, work to last 4 sts, k2tog, k2. When working shaping for back neck, leave the 32 sts at center back on spare needle. Cont

with neck shapings, each side separately, as indicated on chart, then cast off when all rows are completed.

LEFT FRONT

(Use right-hand part of chart only.)

Using 3mm needles and col A, cast on 74 sts. Working in moss st, work 1 row, then dec 1 st at center front edge of next and every foll alt row 8 times (66 sts).

Change to 3.75mm needles and work straight in st st until work measures 9½ in. [20½ in.] from cast-on edge. Foll chart, work the 72 rows, foll

JACKET CHART: BACK AND FRONTS

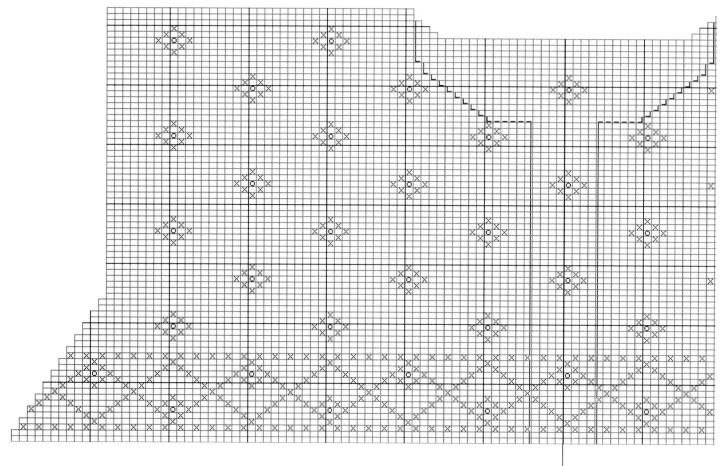

Left front ——————— Right front

the lower neckline for front and dec at armhole as follows: k2, sl 1, k1, psso, work to end. Leave the 6 sts at neck edge on spare needle.

RIGHT FRONT

(Use left-hand part of chart only.)
Work as for left front, but when starting to work from chart and with RS facing, work as follows:

ROW 1 Start with st 75 and work across row, ending with st 140. Dec at armhole by working to last 4 sts, k2tog, k2.

Note: When starting the right front, make sure that dec are on the center front edge of the jacket, the opposite side as the dec on the left front.

SLEEVES

Using 3mm needles and col A, cast on 55 sts and work 16 rows in moss st. Change to 3.75mm needles and work 13 rows in beadwork over these 55 sts, inc 1 st at both ends of the first and every foll fourth row until there are 115 sts. Foll rows 3 to 15 inclusive of chart, working over sts 6

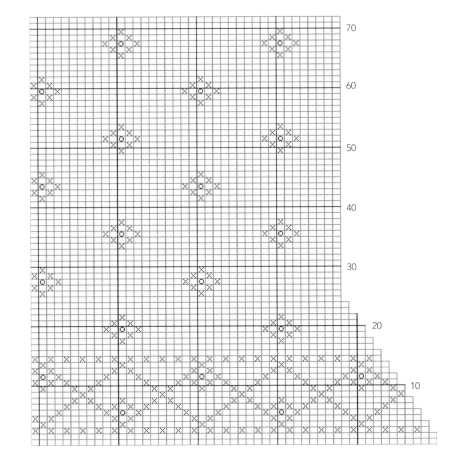

JACKET STITCH KEY

X   Position of bead. Add the beads with a slipstitch. On a RS or a WS row, work to a bead position, put the yarn to RS of work, bring the bead up, and sl the next st. Cont in st st. The strand at the front of the slipped st holds the bead.

to 62 on first row and adding more of the chart as you inc. Cont working in st st, inc 1 st at both ends of set rows until work measures 16½ in. from cast-on edge and ends with a WS row. Foll chart, work as follows over rows 3 to 15 inclusive:

KNIT ROWS Work the last 11 sts, work sts 14 to 33 inclusive 5 times across row, work the first 2 sts.

PURL ROWS Work the first 2 sts, work sts 14 to 33 inclusive 5 times across row, work the first 11 sts.
Keep patt correct as you inc to 115 sts. When 13 rows are completed, cast off evenly and loosely.

FRONT BANDS

With RS facing and using 3mm needles and col A, pick up and knit 90 [156] sts along front edge (to evenly distribute the sts, divide the front edge of jacket into quarters and mark). Pick up 22 [39] sts evenly over 2 sections and 23 [39] sts over the rem 2 sections. Make sure the band fits snugly.

LEFT BAND Working in moss st, inc 1 st at start of next and every alt row 8 times. Cast off neatly.

RIGHT BAND Working in moss st, inc 1 st at end of next and every alt row 8 times. Cast off neatly.

NECKBAND

Join shoulders using a small, neat backstitch on edge of work so that the cast-off edge does not show on RS.
With RS facing and using 3mm needles and col A, start at the right front edge. Pick up and knit 9 sts from top of band; 6 sts from spare needle; 22 sts up to shoulder seam; 3 sts down back neck; 32 sts from spare needle at center back; 3 sts up other side back neck; 22 sts down left side front neck; 6 sts from st holder at center front; and 9 sts from top of left front band (112 sts). Working in moss st, work 5 rows. On sixth row, introduce a bead on every purl st on the RS. Work a further 2 rows, then cast off.

FINISHING

Use a small, neat backstitch on very edge of work for seams. Set in sleeves, placing the cast-off edge of the sleeve along the armhole edge (including the dec edge). The 13 rows of patt on sleeve should match up with those at start of armhole. Join side and sleeve seams in one line. Carefully sew miters at center front using a neat slipstitch.
Attach the frog fastener where the neckband meets the fronts.

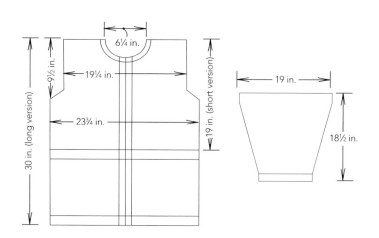

HAT

BEADS

Mother-of-pearl, sequins, and beads
as desired

SIZE

One size

MAKING THE HAT

Make large knitted pieces of felt in each col on a
knitting machine by casting on 200 sts and
working 72 in. per col. Make 2 pieces in the
main col (144 in.) and 1 piece in the contrast col
for underneath the brim. (There is no need to
cast off in between cols or at the end, as you
can cut the fabric without it fraying.) Release
the fabric from the knitting machine and cut it
into pieces of 72 in. The pieces must be
separated because they will felt together if left
in one piece.

If you do not have a knitting machine, you can
recycle your old sweaters by shrinking them in the
washing machine, thereby felting them.

Felt the pieces two at a time in the washing
machine at 140°F. Add powdered detergent and
an old towel, which provides friction and speeds
up the felting process. You may need to put
some pieces through twice, but usually wool will
felt after only one wash. **Note:** Do not use
machine-washable yarn that has been coated
with silicone because it will not felt.

Dry the pieces on a radiator or in a dryer.

Cut out 2 pieces of pattern 1 for the brim, 1 in
each col. Cut out 1 piece each of patterns 2 and
3 for the crown in the main col.

Join back seams by hand on each brim piece,
using an invisible edge-to-edge stitch. Similarly,
join the back seam on pattern 2 to make
another circle. Embroider this side piece using a
neat chainstitch (it can be embroidered with the
Banjara sweater motif or another favorite
pattern), and apply mother-of-pearl, sequins,
and beads. You can also use offcuts of felt as
appliquéd designs and chainstitch them in place.
Place the two brim pieces together (the contrast
col will be on the inside of hat) and blanket
stitch together around the outside edge. Top-
stitch the brim on a sewing machine, running
concentric circles from the outside edge (starting just inside blanket stitch) to center every ¼ in.
Blanket stitch the top of the crown to the
embroidered side piece (seam to be on RS),
and similarly blanket stitch this to the inside
edge of the brim.

YARN

Rowan 4-ply Botany, knitted on knitting
machine, then felted in washing machine.
Choose 2 cols to match your sweater.

Banjara hat

HAT PATTERN 1

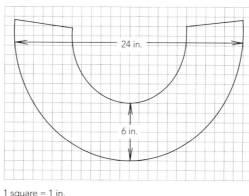

24 in.

6 in.

1 square = 1 in.

HAT PATTERN 3

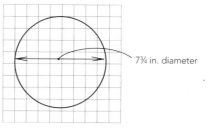

7¾ in. diameter

1 square = 1 in.

HAT PATTERN 2

4½ in.

22½ in.

1 square = 1 in.

YARN SOURCES

Rowan yarns are available from fine yarn stores around the world. For information on retailers that stock these yarns, contact the following national distributors.

UNITED STATES

Westminster Fibers, Inc.
5 Northern Boulevard
Amherst, New Hampshire 03031
Phone: (603) 886-5041 or (603) 886-5043
Fax: (603) 886-1056

CANADA

Diamond Yarn
9697 St. Laurent
Montreal, Quebec H3L 2N1
Phone: (514) 388-6188

UNITED KINGDOM

Rowan
Green Lane Mill
Holmfirth, West Yorks HD7 IRW
Phone: 01484 681881

AUSTRALIA

MacEwen Enterprises
1/178 Cherry Lane
Laverton North, Victoria 3026
Phone: 03 9369 3988 or (800) 816-539

BELGIUM

Hedera
Pleinstraat 68
3001 Leuven
Phone: (016) 23 21 89

DENMARK

Filcolana A/S
Hagemannsvej 26-28, Postboks 151
DK 8600 Silkeborg
Phone: 86 81 02 11

FRANCE

Elle Tricote
52 Rue Principale
67300 Schiltigheim
Phone: 03 88 62 6531

GERMANY

Wolle & Design
Wolfshovener Strasse 76
52428 Julich-Stetternich
Phone: 02461/54735

JAPAN

Diakeito Co. Ltd.
2-3-11 Senba-Higashi
Minoh City, Osaka 562
Phone: 0727 27 6604

MAIL ORDER KNIT KITS FROM JEAN MOSS

ALBION SWEATER	£74	**HAUSA PILLOW**	£49
ALBION PILLOW	£48	**HAUSA SOCKS**	£22
BALUCH JACKET	£78	**KUBA TUNIC**	£65 (WOOL), £78 (COTTON)
BALUCH SWEATER	£66	**KUBA CARDIGAN**	£78
BALUCH PILLOW	£55	**KUBA PILLOW**	£32
BALUCH SOCKS	£22	**KUBA SOCKS**	£21
BANJARA SWEATER (BEADS NOT INCLUDED) £60		**LISDOONVARNA JACKET**	£60
DAJAN JACKET	£88	**MAYA JACKET**	£75
DAJAN VEST	£64	**MAYA PILLOW**	£39
DAJAN SLIPPER SOCKS	£26	**SHOOWA SWEATER**	£65 (COTTON OR WOOL)
DAJAN SERAPÉ £80 (WOOL), £153 (SILK)		**SHOOWA WAISTCOAT**	£59
HAUSA JACKET	£85	**THROWS**	PRICES UPON REQUEST
HAUSA SWEATER	£81		

Kits contain Rowan yarn, handmade Nepalese buttons where applicable, and pattern. Slight variations of color may occur when certain shades are occasionally unavailable. While I try to maintain the listed prices, please note that during the life of the book prices may be subject to increase without notice. Prices are quoted in sterling. Credit card orders from the United States and elsewhere can be made in sterling. This helps keep the cost to you as low as possible.
Ready-made items can be specially ordered. Ask for details.

ORDER FORM

DESIGN	COLORWAY		PRICE	
Please add £5 p&p + £3 for each extra item				
		Total		

name

address

postal/zip code phone

method of payment

Credit card | | | | | | | | | | | | | | | |

☐ VISA

☐ ACCESS Expiration date   Name on card

☐ MASTERCARD

☐ DELTA

Signature (as shown on card)

Check or postal order (UK only) payable to Jean Moss.

Mail to: JEAN MOSS, 17 CLIFTON DALE, YORK YO3 6LJ, UNITED KINGDOM
Phone/fax: 01904 646282; e-mail: moss@dircon.co.uk
If you do not wish to cut out this page, please photocopy it.

Book publisher: JIM CHILDS

Acquisitions editor: JOLYNN GOWER

Publishing coordinator: SARAH COE

Editor: DIANE SINITSKY

Designer/layout artist: AMY BERNARD

Photographers: JACK DEUTSCH,
SCOTT PHILLIPS (PP. 10, 24, 38, 84, 98, 116, AND 136)

Illustrator: ROSALIE VACCARO

Typefaces: LITHOS, PALATINO, AVENIR

Paper: 70-LB. PATINA

Printer: QUEBECOR PRINTING/KINGSPORT, KINGSPORT, TENNESSEE